Enjoy the walk, and may the sunshine all day, the wind at your back and your feet comfy in your boots.

Happy walking!

John N. Merrill

Happy walking! John N. Merrill

Something to ponder.

As we walk around this amazing world, we take for granted the stunning diversity of life and nature. We pass the slopes of mountains and the river valleys. We see birds, insects, animals and all the kaleidoscope of flowers and trees. But let's stop for a moment and just stand in awe of this plethora of sights. However hard we, as humans try, we cannot match the magnificence that our eyes see. Whether you are spiritual or not, you cannot ignore or be moved to wonder at the incredible work of a higher dimension - the divine.

While many would say this is evolution, there still has be "someone", who first thought up the flower, tree, bird, animal, and landscape. You only have to gaze at a small mountain flower and see the delicate stems and petals made to perfection. Whilst the earth's movement have created our landscape, the forces of the divine have been at work to help create that breathtaking view. We on the other-hand have been given eyes and feelings, so that we can appreciate and stand in awe at the sight before us.

So as we wander down a path in woodland or high mountains, where the whole spectrum of life is laid out for us to see. Lets give eternal thanks for being able to walk and see these things first hand. To be able to touch, feel and appreciate the work of the divine, makes the effort more than worthwhile. So, as you walk, stop and ponder at the never ending variety of sights and smells that confront us on each stride we take.

John N. Merrill 2014

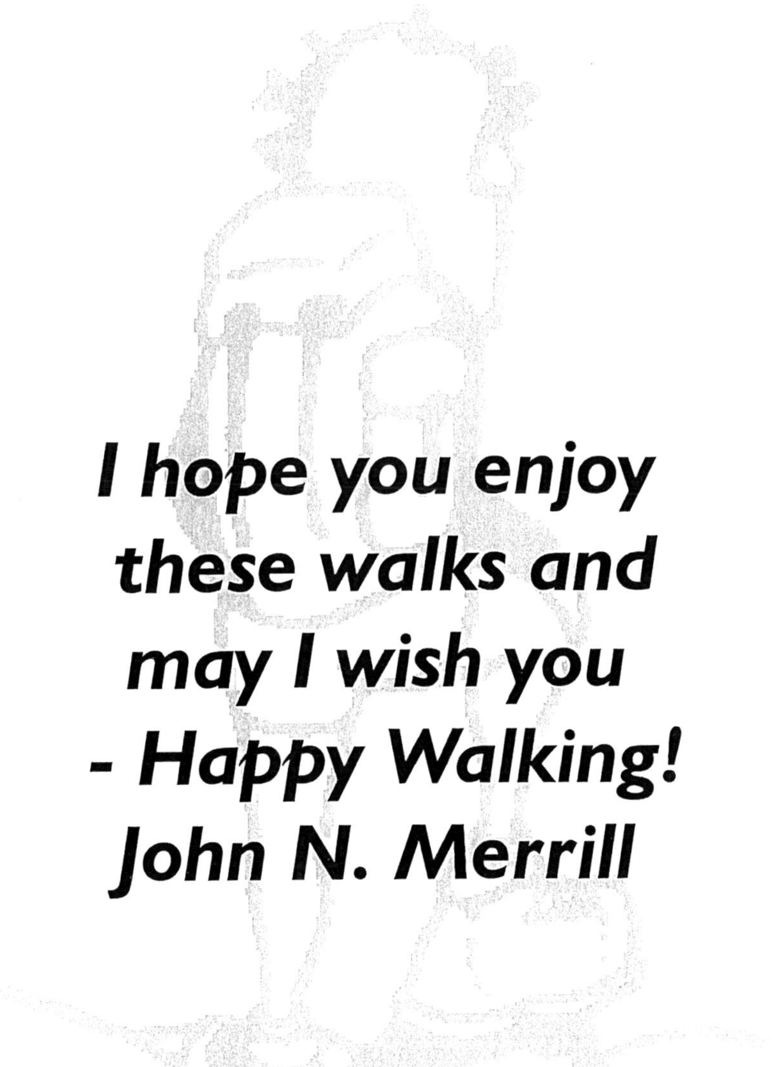

I hope you enjoy these walks and may I wish you - Happy Walking!

John N. Merrill

Walks in the London Borough of ENFIELD

by Revd. John N. Merrill

Maps, pencil sketches, Chinese Brush paintings and photographs by John N. Merrill

"I hike the paths and trails of the world for others to enjoy."

The London Borough Walks Series - Vol One.

THE JOHN MERRILL FOUNDATION
& MINISTRY

2013

THE JOHN MERRILL FOUNDATION

32, Holmesdale, Waltham Cross, Hertfordshire, England. EN8 8QY

Tel/Fax - 01992-762776
E-mail - john@johnmerrillwalkguides.co.uk
www. johnmerrillwalkguides.co.uk
www.thejohnmerrillministry.co.uk
www.londoninterfaithchurch.co.uk

A catalogue record for this book is available from the British Library.

Conceived, edited, typset and designed by *The John Merrill Foundation*
Printed and handmade by ***John N. Merrill.***
Book layout and cover design by ***John N. Merrill***

ISBN 978 - 0-9556511-2-0
First Published - October 2007. Reprinted, enlarged & Revised - August 2013.
Special limited edition.

Typeset in Humanst521 - bold, italic, and plain 11pt, 14pt and 18pt
Main titles in 18pt .**Humanst521 Bd BT** by John Merrill in Adobe Pagemaker on a iMac.

Please note - *The maps in this guide are purely illustrative. You are encouraged to use the appropriate 1:25,000 O.S. Explorer map as detailed on each walk.*

John Merrill confirms he has walked all the routes in this book and detailed what he found. Meticulous research has been undertaken to ensure that this publication is highly accurate at the time of going to press. The publishers, however, cannot be held responsible for alterations, errors, omissions, or for changes in details given. They would welcome information to help keep the book up to date.

The John Merrill Foundation maintains the John Merrill Library and archives and administers the worldwide pubishing rights of John Merrill's works in all media formats.

Printed on paper from a 100% sustainable forest.
The John Merrill Foundation plants sufficient trees through the Woodland Trust to replenish the trees used in its publications.

The author at Assisi, after walking The Camino di Assisi - 320 km. in Italy - July 2012.

ABOUT THE AUTHOR

Over the last 46 years John Merrill has walked over 206,000 miles, - more than ten times around the world - wearing out more than 1,000 pairs of socks and 119 pairs of boots in the process. He has completed a remarkable and unequalled number of marathon walks - walking more than 28 miles per day on average - including being the first person to walk around Britain - 7,000 miles - in ten months. He has walked across Europe, Africa, India, Nepal, Asia, America, and along the great trails of America and Canada. He has completed numerous Pilgrim routes to Santiago de Compostela, Canterbury, Walsingham, St. Albans, to Assis and Cathar' ways and to Trondheim in Norway. Many more pilgrimages and marathons are planned.

He is acknowledged as Britain's Greatest Walker.

He has written more than 400 guidebooks to his walks, most of which he prints and publishes himself. After his coast walk he realised the fame game prevented his from doing what he was destined to do, and that was to simply walk and write. He purposefully left the stage and concentrated on what he wanted to do. He does not consult anyone, promote or seek publicity; preferring to follow his own quiet spiritual path through life. This means he can write a book, on average one every month. He is not beholden to anyone, just a free spirit, with no staff, agents or editors. As a result he is not rich in money terms but in life and places walked to, a millionaire.

He is not a loner, quite the reverse, but to get the material and accomplish his walks - he who travels alone, travels fastest. And, by going alone you never forget. He is guided and has a very deep spiritual faith and has never come to any harm or put a foot wrong. The only way to be close to nature and see its huge variety is by walking; no other sport/exercise gives you that connectedness to the earth. He does no research beforehand, preferring to walk around the corner and come to a church, historic house, sacred site etc., and discover for himself their secrets. To be aware of what's next is to dampen the impact.

" A journey of a thousand miles, begins with a single step."
Lao Tzu (The Tao Te Ching).
"The walk begins when you close the door behind you" - JNM 5/2013

I am on a long journey, which continues daily - one life is not enough.

"I cannot be defined,
No Label sticks to me,
No pigeon hole do I fit.
I am connected to everything,
I am part of the whole.
A part has no meaning on its own"
(©John Merill 17/9/2010)

My religion is simple - *"I love everything and everyone"*

On July 17th. 2010 John was Ordained as an Interfaith Minister - *"He embraces and honours all faiths."*

See - ***www.thejohnmerrillministry.co.uk***
www.londoninterfaithchurch.co.uk

CONTENTS

Page No.

Introduction 9

About the walks 10

The Art of Walking the John Merrill Way 11

Observe the Country Code 12

Equipment Notes - Some personal thoughts 13

Enfield Town Park & New River Loop - 2 miles 14

Brief History about the New River 18

Enfield Parks and New River - 7 miles 20

The New River in Enfield - 8 miles 26

Around Trent Country Park - 4 miles 32

Forty Hall, Whitewebbs Park and Hilly Fields Park - 4 1/2 miles 36

Southgate - Grovelands Park - 2 miles 42

Walking the Streets of Edmonton - 5 miles 46

The Pymmes Brook Trail - 10 miles 58

The London Loop, in Enfield - 10 miles 66

The River Lee Navigation - Pickett's Lock to Enfield Lock - 5 miles 72

Enfield Town & Forty Hill Historical Walk - 4 miles 76

Ponders End, River Lee, Brimsdown & Durants Park - 6 miles 88

Go for it! - The Enfield Circular Challenge Walk - 25 miles 94

Walk Record Chart 97

Walk Badge Order Form 98

The London Borough Walks Series 99

Other London Walk books by John Merrill 101

Other books by John Merrill 105

Why I Walk 107

FORTY HALL - Built in 1629 for Sir Nicholas Rainton; Lord Mayor of London and President of St. Bartholomew's Hospital. The hall, a fine Jacobean Mansion, is known for traditional compact design, plaster ceilings, panelled rooms and walled gardens. In 1787 the hall and estate were auctioned, with the hall being bought by Edmund Armstrong. By 1895 it was owned by Major Henry Bowles MP for Enfield. In 1951 Enfield Urban District Council bought the hall and grounds and converted them into a museum; a visit is highly recommended.

My thanks – I would like to thank the staff of several Enfield Libraries who have been most helpful is finding the story or history of a particular building or park. Notably, Ordance Road Library; Enfield Central Library; Edmonton Library and Waltham Cross Library (Hertfordshire). Also, but not least, the staff at the Local History Unit at Palmers Green.

ENFIELD FACTS - In 2008 the population of the borough was 285,100. Among the famous born here are, singer Amy Winehouse from Southgate and both show host Bruce Forsythe and actor David Jason come from Edmonton. In 2008 the borough was twinned with Halandri, Greece and Sariyer, Turkey, reflecting the borough's main ethnic communities. The two other twins are Galdbeck, Germany and Courbevoie, France.

INTRODUCTION

My passport states I was born in London, but I was only here for my first nine months before being adopted and brought up in the City of Sheffield. Only recently have I returned to my birthplace, and as is my vocation, began to explore the area on foot. First I explored the River Lee Navigation, then the London Loop - which I walked all the way round - and the New River. I walked on along the Pymmes Brook Trail before exploring the parks and towns of the borough. The more I walked the more appreciative I became of the area.

Whilst there are only about 66 kilometres (40 miles) of footpaths in the borough, this does not reflect the amount of walking there is. Grovelands Park was a delightful surprise, as was the nearby Village Pound; a countryside survivor in London's suburbia. Perhaps "King" of all, Forty Hall is an exceptional building and a fine place to walk. Trent Country Park is particularly attractive with extensive unspoilt woodland and lakes. Street walking is part of the London walking scene, and a walk around Edmonton brings you too many fine buildings and much history. Enfield has an old loop of the New River, which combined with the Town Park, makes a short figure of eight walk.

In the west the 10 mile Pymmes Brook Trail passes through several beautiful parks on its way to Pickett's Lock. Here you can walk the River Lee Navigation, which proved a vital link to London during World War 11 and where narrowboats still meander. Wildfowl are numerous along its banks, as they are in the parks. The northern end of the borough is where the London Loop passes through the rolling countryside of Enfield Chase and Hilly Fields Park, before gaining the River Lee Navigation at Enfield Lock.

These ten walks illustrate the variety of walking in the borough and I hope they encourage you to slip on your pack and lace up your walking boots and set off and explore your neighbourhood. I am sure you will be surprised at what it has to offer. Walking is the only way to explore and get to know the area. For those wanting a challenge, there is a 25 mile walk at the end!

Happy walking!
John Merrill

ABOUT THE WALKS
- some general comments.

Whilst every care is taken detailing and describing the walks in this book, it should be borne in mind that the countryside changes by the seasons and the work of man. I have described the walk to the best of my ability, detailing what I have found actually on the walk in the way of stiles and signs. Obviously with the passage of time stiles become broken or replaced by a ladder stile , a small gate or a kissing gate. Signs too have a habit of being broken or pushed over - vandelism. All the route follow rights of way and only on rare occasions will you have to overcome obstacles in its path, such as a blown down tree, barbed wire fence or an electric fence. On rare occasions rights of way are rerouted and these ammendments are included in the next edition. Inns have a frustrating habit of changing their name, then back to the original one!

All rights of way have colour coded arrows; on marker posts, stiles/gates and trees; these help you to show the direction of the right of way -

Yellow - Public footpath.
Blue - Public bridleway.
Red - Byway open to all traffic (BOAT).
Black - Road used as a public path (RUPP).
White - Concessionary and Permissive path

The seasons bring occasional problems whilst out walking which should also be borne in mind. In the height of summer paths become overgrown and you may have to fight your way through in a few places. In low lying areas the fields are often full of crops, and although the pathline goes straight across it may be more practical to walk round the field edge to get to the next stile or gate. In summer the ground is generally dry but in autumn and winter, especially because of our climate, the surface can be decidedly wet and slippery; sometimes even gluttonous mud!

These comments are part of countryside walking which help to make your walk more interesting or briefly frustrating. Standing in a track up to your ankles in mud might not be funny at the time but upon reflection was one of the highlights of the walk!

The mileage for each section is based on three calculations -

1. pedometer and stepometer readings.
2. the route map measured on the map.
3. the time I took for the walk.

I believe the figure stated for each section to be very accurate but we all walk differently and not always in a straight line! The time allowed for each section is on the generous side and does not include pub stops etc. The figure is based on the fact that on average a person walks 2 1/2 miles an hours but less in hilly terrain. Allow 20 minutes to walk a mile; ten minutes for 1/2 mile and five minutes for 1/4 mile. On average you will walk 2,000 strides to a mile - an average stride is 31 inches..

"For every mile you walk, you extend your life by 21 minutes"

The Art of Walking the John Merrill Way.

1. Always set off in the clothes you plan to wear all day, given the weather conditions. Only on sudden changes in the weather will I stop and put on a waterproof or warmer clothing.

2. Set off at a steady comfortable pace, which you can maintain all day. You should end the walk as fresh as when as you started.

3. Maintain your pace and don't stop. Stopping for any period of time disrupts your rhythm and takes upwards of a mile to settle back down into the flow/ease of movement.

4. Switch off your mobile phone and music centre, and listen and enjoy the countryside - the smells of the flowers, bird song, the rustle of the leaves and the tinkling stream.

5. Ignore the mileage and ascents - don't tick of the miles, just concentrate on what the walk's goal is. To think otherwise slows you down and makes the walk a struggle rather than a joy. In a similar vein, when ascending just keep a steady pace and keep going. To stop is to disrupt the flow and make the ascent interminable.

6. Whilst a walk is a challenge to complete, it is not just exercise. You should enjoy the world around you; the flowers, birds, wildlife and nature and look at and explore the historical buildings and church's that you pass. All are part of life's rich tapestry.

7. Remember that for every mile that you walk, you extend your life by 21 minutes.

8. A journey of a 1,000 miles begins with a single step and a mile requires 2,000 strides.

"The expert traveller leaves no footprints."
Lao Tzu.

Follow the Countryside Code.

* Be safe - plan ahead and follow any signs.

* Leave gates and property as you find them.

* Protect plants and animals, and take your litter home.

* Keep dogs under close control.

* Consider other people.

EQUIPMENT NOTES

Today there is a bewildering variety of walking gear, much is superfluous to general walking in Britain. As a basic observation, people over dress for the outdoors. Basically equipment should be serviceable and do the task. I don't use walking poles; humans were built to walk with two legs! The following are some of my thoughts gathered from my walking experiences.

BOOTS - For summer use and day walking I wear lightweight boots. For high mountains and longer trips I prefer a good quality boot with a full leather upper, of medium weight, traditional style ,with a vibram sole. I always add a foam cushioned insole to help cushion the base of my feet.

SOCKS - I generally wear two thick pairs as this helps minimise blisters. The inner pair are of loop stitch variety and approximately 80% wool. The outer are also a thick pair of approximately 80% wool. I often wear double inner socks, which minimise blisters.

CLOTHES & WATERPROOFS - for general walking I wear a T shirt or cotton shirt with a cotton wind jacket on top, and shorts - even in snow! You generate heat as you walk and I prefer to layer my clothes to avoid getting too hot. Depending on the season will dictate how many layers you wear. In soft rain I just use my wind jacket for I know it quickly dries out. In heavy or consistent rain I slip on a poncho, which covers me and my pack and allows air to circulate, while keeping me dry. Only in extreme conditions will I don over-trousers, much preferring to get wet and feel comfortable. I never wear gaiters, except when cross country skiing, or in snow and glacier crossings. I find running shorts and sleeveless T shirts ideal for summer.

FOOD - as I walk I carry bars of chocolate, for they provide instant energy and are light to carry. In winter a flask of hot coffee is welcome. I never carry water and find no hardship from not doing so, but this is a personal matter! From experience I find the more I drink the more I want and sweat. You should always carry some extra food such as trail mix & candy bars etc., for emergencies. Full milk is a very underestimated source of food and liquid.

RUCKSACKS - for day walking I use a rucksack of about 30/40 litre capacity and although it leaves excess space it does mean that the sac is well padded, with an internal frame and padded shoulder straps, chest strap and waist strap. Inside apart from the basics for one day, in winter I carry gloves, wear a hat/cap and carry a spare pullover and a pair of socks.

MAP & COMPASS - when I am walking I always have the relevant map - preferably 1:25,000 scale - open in my hand. This enables me to constantly check that I am walking the right way. In case of bad weather I carry a compass, which once mastered gives you complete confidence in thick cloud or mist - you should always know where you are; I have a built in direction finder! Map reading and compass work is a skill and should be learnt. With modern technology you can now downloaded OS maps to your phone, record your walk, mileage, calories, steps taken, walking speed and time taken.

ENFIELD TOWN PARK & NEW RIVER LOOP - 2 MILES

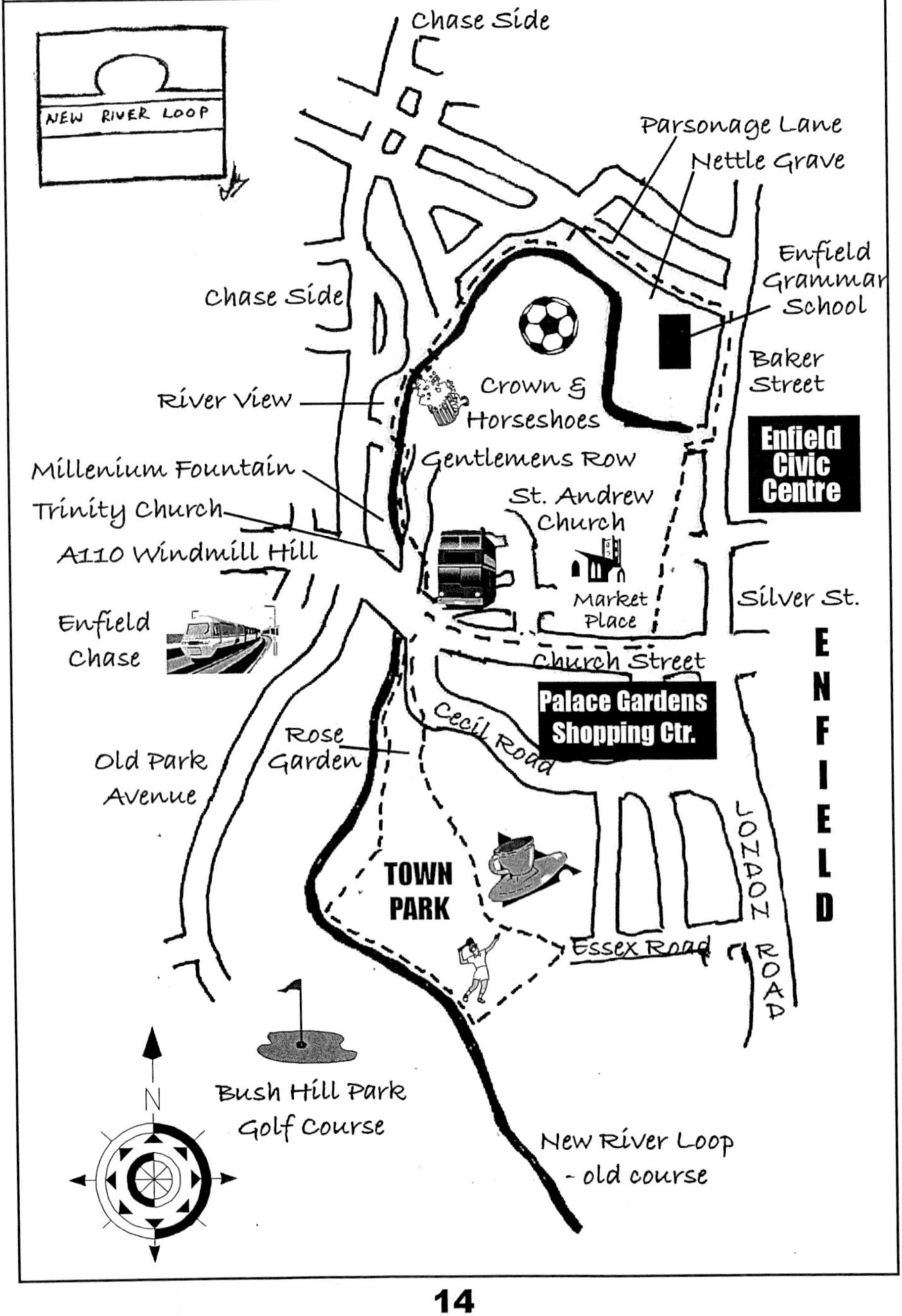

ENFIELD TOWN PARK & NEW RIVER LOOP - 2 MILES - allow 1 1/2 hours 1 or 2 walks

ABOUT THE WALKS - The whole walk is in the shape of a figure 8 and can either be walked as a whole or as two separate walks - Walk one - 1 1/4 miles and Walk 2 - 3/4 mile. Whilst the walks start and ends at the bus turnaround - Little Park Gardens; you can start from Enfield Chase Station, a few yards west of the start, up Windmill Hill. There are also car parks off Cecil Road and bus stops on both Church Street and Cecil Road. The basic aim of the walk is to follow a section of the now abandoned loop of the New River, at the same time seeing some of central Enfield's historical places. In the pavement at frequent intervals can be seen the New River Loop emblem.

Walk one - 1 1/4 miles - Basic route - Bus turnaround close to junction of Cecil Road and Church Street - Gentlemen's Row - New River Loop - River View - Parsonage Lane - Baker Street - Enfield Civic Centre - St. Andrew's Church - Church Street - Bus turnaround.

Inns - Stag Inn, Little park Gardens. Crown & Horseshoes Inn, River View. King's Head, Market Place.

Cafe - Church Street, Enfield.

WALKING INSTRUCTIONS - From the bus turnaround, cross the road and walk along Gentleman's Row on the immediate right of the Stag Inn. In a few yards reach Clarendon House and bear left through the car park to the New River. Turn right beside it with the gardens and Millennium Fountain on the otherside. Continue to a footbridge and cross and turn right along River View with the river now on your right. This stretch by the houses is perhaps the prettiest walk in Enfield. At the end by the Crown & Horseshoe Inn, cross the river - bridge dated 1841 - and turn left, keeping it on your left. In a short distance cross another bridge and continue with the river loop on your right. Follow the path which later leaves the river to gain Parsonage Lane. Turn right and as you near school buildings (Enfield Grammar School) on your right, through the railings can be seen be seen the tombstone of the dog, Nettle. He died aged 11 and was the faithful dog of Colin.......

Soon after turn right along Baker Street and when opposite the Police Station and Enfield Civic Centre, at the start of Silver Street, turn right into a No Through Road - Portcullis Lodge Road. (Just ahead along Silver Street is White Lodge; now a surgery but was where the founder and publisher of Whitaker's Almanac lived.) On the immediate right is the loop of the New River. In a few yards at the road barrier turn left along a fenced path which brings you to the parish church of St. Andrew's. Walk through the graveyard and onto the Market Place, with the Kings Head Inn on the right. Continue to the main road and shops of Church Street. Turn right and follow the road back to the bus turnaround area, with Trinity Church on the corner.

Walk Two - 3/4 mile - Basic route - Bus turnaround (Little park Gardens) - New River Loop - Town Park - Cecil Road - Bus turnaround.

Cafe - In Town Park.

WALKING INSTRUCTIONS - Cross the road to your left and in a few yards left again into the Town Park, with the New River on your right. Keep beside it for some six minutes to a bridge over it; on your right is a "lake", Carr's Basin made in the 18th. century. Do not cross but continue on the path with the river on your right and the park on your left. Continue to the corner of the park and turn left, leaving the river, and following a tarmaced path. Pass tennis courts on your left and soon after reach the parks gates at the end of Essex Road. Turn half left to continue on another tarmaced path in the middle of the park to pass water ponds and Park Cafe. Keep ahead and soon walk through a rose garden and onto the gate entrance before Cecil Road. Walk to the road and turn left, passing Enfield Central Library on the right, before regaining your earlier path with the bus turnaround on the right.

GENTLEMAN'S ROW - A row of delightful houses and by far the most attractive street in Enfield. The Georgian building - No 1. is now Enfield's Registry Office. For a greater insight into this row see the book - *"A Portrait of Gentleman's Row"* .Published by the Enfield Preservation Society. 1986.

See separate walk to the rear of the book, on page 76 and onwards, for a more detailed look at this row and other Enfield Historical buildings.

ENFIELD GRAMMAR SCHOOL - The original part was built in the 18th. century and known as Enfield Court. The building was converted to a school in 1924 and the former grounds are now the sports area.

ST. ANDREW'S CHURCH - The tower and nave date back to 14th. century, with the north aisle built in the late 15th. century. The south aisle was rebuilt in 1826. Inside are several brasses and monuments including a large one to Sir Nicholas Rainton,his wife, Rebecca, and children; who built Forty Hall.

MARKET PLACE - The market dates from 1616, and the current design dates from 1632 and was where the stocks and whipping post once were, for those who were caught poaching on Enfield Chase. The central open Market House was built in 1904, to commemorate King Edward VII coronation. It sits on the site of the market cross. The cast iron water pump was replaced here in 1979. The King's Head Inn was built in 1899, replacing the former 17th. century inn. An inn on this site dates back to 1516.

CHURCH STREET - The Palace Shopping Centre occupies part of the site of Enfield Palace, which dated back to Medieval times. A plaque on Barclays Bank records this was where the World's first Cash Dispenser was installed on June 27th. 1967. The Goose at the George Inn was rebuilt in 1895; originally known as The George, there has been an inn on this site since 1548. The tall building on the right, was Enfield's tallest building, built in 1897. The drinking fountain with tri-corn lights was started in 1884 but was not completed until 1885, because of funding problems.

TOWN PARK - Formerly the grounds of Chase Side House. Officially opened as the Town Park on July 30th. 1902.

ENFIELD'S CREST - The red unusual animal is the crest of the Irish family of Kelly. It has a fox's head and ears; a wolf's body, hind legs and tail; and an eagle's shanks and talons for its forelegs.

NEW RIVER
- some brief history notes.

As many historical notice boards along the river state - It is not a river, nor is it new. It is a remarkable piece of 17th. century engineering to bring clean water to London, some 400 years ago. Originally 40 miles long from Chadwell Spring near Hertford, to the New River Head in Islington, London; close to Saddler's Wells Theatre. The "river" hugs the 100 foot contour line, often doing loops to maintain height, such as around Forty Hall and Enfield Town. Today it is 24 miles long, with the loops omitted by taking the water through pipes and tunnels. The aim behind the 100 foot contour line, was so water could then be gravity fed to the houses of the City of London.

A water channel was proposed in 1600 and an Act of 1606 basically set up the scheme. Originally Edmund Colhurst, who had proposed the channel, was to undertake the task. However concerns over financing, the council accepted an offer from Hugh Myddleton, a welshman, who was a London goldsmith and a former M.P. He agreed to finance the project himself and complete it on four years. Hugh Myddleton was knighted in October 1662 and died on December 10th. 1631 and a statue to him can be seen in Islington close to Camden Antique Market.

Work began at Chadwell Spring on April 21st. 1609 and was completed more than four years later on September 29th. 1613 - the Lord Mayor of London officially opened the waterway on this day. The cost of construction is believed to be £18,527. 0d. 1d. The "river" was basically 10 feet wide and 4 feet deep. Puddled clay was used as a liner to make it waterproof. Over its 40 mile length the water falls 18 ft. - 5 1/2 inches a mile. 157 bridges were built along its path for roads and paths across the "river".

In the first year 175 houses were using the water supply and the following year this had doubled. By 1809 it was 59,058 houses and by 1834 this had risen to 73,212. As the demand for water increased reservoirs were built at Cheshunt and the East and West Reservoirs at Stoke Newington.

The New River is still used by Thames Water Board; the river being fed mostly by the River Lee, which rises near Luton. Originally the New River was fed by the springs at Chadwell and Amwell, who combined provided a maximum of 10 megalitres a day. A statue in 1738 allowed upto 102 megalitres to be taken from the River Lee. More than century later these amounts were doubled. Today, more than 38 million gallons of water, a day, is brought to London along this "river."

For a full in depth look at the New River, see Michael Essex-Lopresti book - ***"Exploring The New River."***

New River History Board & local map.

ENFIELD PARKS AND NEW RIVER - 7 MILES

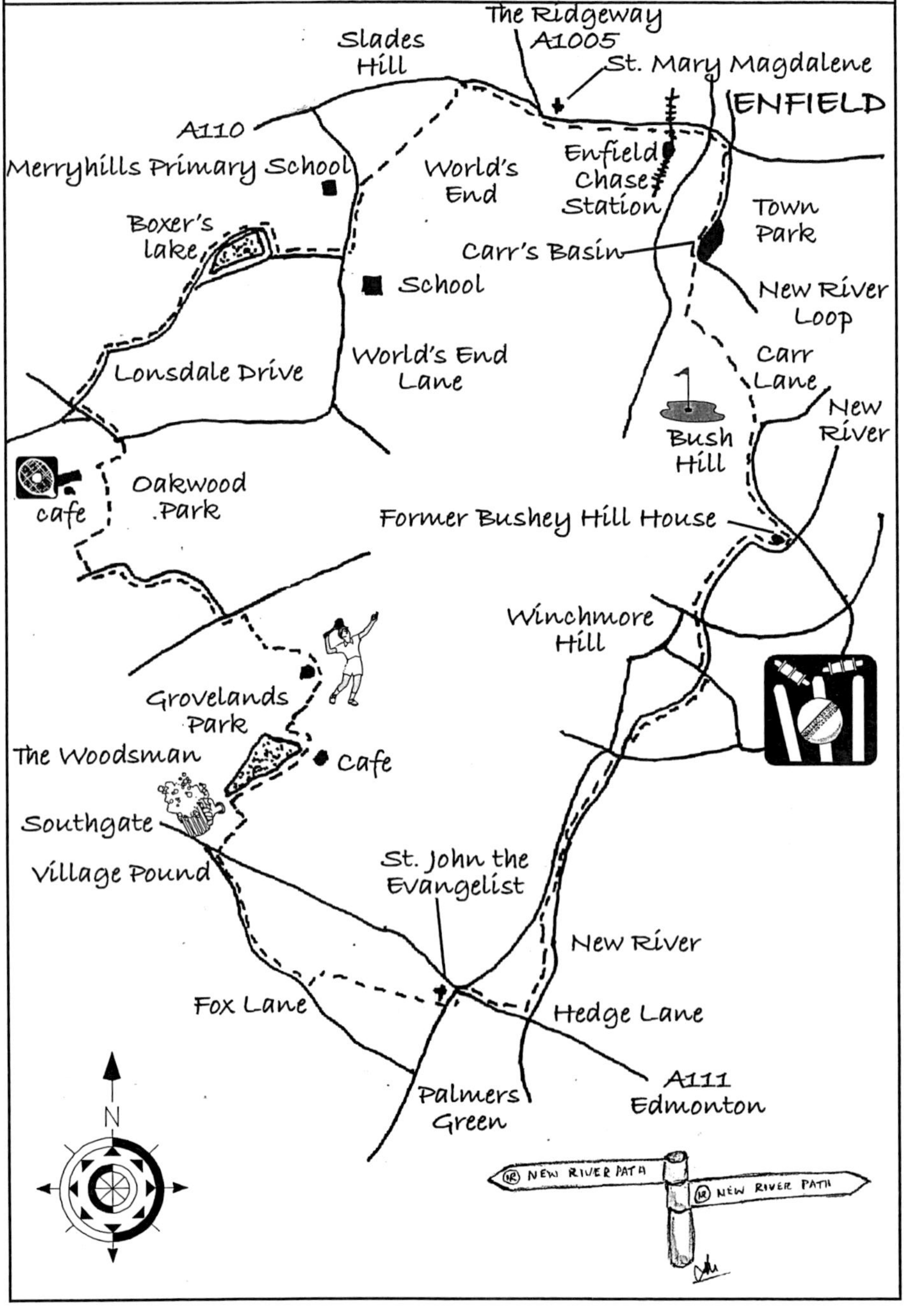

ENFIELD PARKS AND NEW RIVER - 7 MILES - allow 3 hours.

***Basic route** - Enfield Town Park - New River Loop - Carrs Lane - Bushey Hill - New River - Winchmore Hill - Palmers Green - Southgate - Grovelands Park - Oakwood Park - Boxers Lake - Worlds End - Slades Hill - Enfield Town.*

***Map** - O.S. 1:25,000 Explorer Series No. 173 - London North.*

***Start and end** - Enfield Town park, beside Cecil Road and Little Park Gardens, bus turnaround area. You can also reach here from Enfield Chase Railway Station, just up Windmill Hill.*

***Inns** - Orange Tree Inn, Winchmore Hill. The Woodman Inn, Southgate. The Stag Inn, Little Park Gardens, Enfield.*

***Cafe** - Grovelands Park. Oakwood Park, just off the route.*

ABOUT THE WALK - A complete mixture of New River walking, parks and street walking. First you explore the New River Loop in Enfield before picking up the flowing New River and passing the site where Sir Hugh Myddleton, the creator of the New River lived at Bushey Hill House between 1609-1613. You pass the historic Winchmore Hill Cricket Club (1880) before leaving the New River and walking towards Palmers Green. Here you pick up a path which leads you to the historic Southgate Village Pound, before entering Grovelands Park. A short road walk brings you to your next park, Oakwood Park, before walking past Boxer's Lake to World's End Lane. Here you pick up your last path to Slades Hill and descend back to Enfield Town. A surprising walk surrounded by London suburbia.

WALKING INSTRUCTIONS - Starting from opposite Trinity Church and the Stag Inn at the end of the main shopping street, Church Street, in Enfield. Cross the road and take the second path on the righthand side of the New River Loop. Soon pass a large lake - Carr's Basin - and reach a footbridge over the loop. Turn right over the bridge and up the tarmaced and fenced path ascending gently to a T junction. Turn left along Carrs Lane, mostly a footpath, as you pass Bush Hill Park Golf Course on your right. At the end reach the entrance to the golf club at Bush Hill. Turn right along the road and follow it as it curves left and becomes Bush Hill Road. In a short distance pass Cunard Crescent on your right with a blue plaque on the righthand gatepost - "Site of Bush Hill House". Just after go through a green kissing gate on the right and walk beside the New River on your left. Follow it round to steps and descend to Ridge Avenue. Turn left and walk along the road with the New River up on your left to the shops at Masons Corner.

Turn left and in a few yards right to a kissing gate and rejoin walking beside the New River. At the next road turn left and right to continue now with the river on your right. On you left is Winchmore Hill Cricket Club. Follow to the path to a footbridge and cross the river and gain Fords Lane with shops to your right. Cross and bear half left along Farm Road and right again to rejoin the New River. At the next road with the Orange Tree Inn to your left, cross and continue with the New River on your left. Soon after cross Carpenters Gardens road and continue with the river on your left. At the next road turn right to the main road, Greens Lanes, (A105). In a few yards turn left along River Avenue and follow this to the next road, Hedge Lane. Here leave the New River, which is to your left.

Turn right along Hedge Lane and follow it to the cross roads infront of St. John the Evangelist church, Palmers Green. Cross and turn left along Green Lanes. In a few yards just before house no. 501, turn right onto a signed footpath. Keep straight ahead and cross a railway line and three roads before the path turns left to Fox Lane. Turn right and ascend the lane passing Corrib Court on your right. At the end of the road at the junction with The Bourne (Southgate Road), reach the Village Pound. Cross the road and to your left is The Woodmans Inn. Keep straight ahead through the gates into Grovelands Park, along a fenced path with a small golf course on the left. Where the path turns left, turn left and descend the path to the tarmaced path around the lake. Turn right and keep the lake on your left and pass a children's play area and Park Cafe on your right. Follow the tarmaced path left and at the lake overflow turn right and descend the path in woodland to the third bridge on your left. Cross and rejoin a tarmaced path and shortly turn left along it as it ascends gently with tennis courts on your left. Follow it left to the first park entrance on your right.

Turn right out of the park. Cross Park View and keep ahead along Park Gate Road to Winchmore Hill Road. Turn left and in a few yards pass Austen Court on your right. Immediately after turn right, as footpath signed. At the bottom turn left then right to walk along Fountains Crescent. Follow this as it curves left and onto its end, where it turns sharp left. Turn right onto a path and walk past tall oak trees to another road. Cross and keep ahead into Oakwood Park on a tarmaced path. At the next path junction keep straight ahead and at the next turn right. Follow the tarmaced path right then left, passing the lefthand turning to the tennis courts and Park Cafe. Beyond turn right along the parks perimeter and turn left out of the park to Prince George Avenue.

Keep half left along Prince George Avenue and take the second road on your right - Kenwood Avenue. Follow this down and cross a roundabout and continue along Lower Kenwood Avenue. At the bottom turn right along Lonsdale Drive. Where it divides keep to the lefthand side and pass woodland on your right before reaching Boxers Lake. Keep to the lefthand side beside the lake on the right and follow the path around the righthand side to a play area and back to Lonsdale Drive. Turn left to World's End Lane.

Turn left and follow the lane to where it curves left with Merryhills Primary School on the corner. Turn right onto a tarmaced path and walk beside a stream on your right. Pass the end of Slades Rise and keep straight ahead, now ascending to Slades Hill. Turn right and continue ascending to the junction with The Ridgeway Road (A1005) and St. Mary Magdalene church opposite. Turn right and descend Windmill Hill past shops and Enfield Chase Railway Station back to Trinity Church and Little Park Gardens.

WINCHMORE HILL CRICKET CLUB - Dates from 1880. In the early 20th. century it was a popular scene with more than 10,000 attending matches held iover three days in early August.

GROVELANDS PARK - See separate Grovelands Park Walk.

OAKWOOD PARK - once part of the southern end of Enfield Chace. The chace was disafforested in 1777 and in 1791 was divided up with 1,231 acres going to Edmonton, including what is now known as Oakwood Park.. The park was originally known as Oak Lodge and in 1870 was bought by Samuel Sugden, a homeopathic chemist. He enlarged the farmhouse into a large house, which he called Oak Lodge. The building was pulled down in the 1920's and Southgate Council bought the park - 64 acres - for £17,134, in 1927.

BOXERS LAKE - Once this was prt of the South Lodge and Farm estate, but was sold in 1935. More than 1,000 houses were built on the land, but 11 acres of woodland and lake were retained.

WORLD'S END - 19th. century name for an area, which at that time, was the end of known "area" locally; few ventured out into this unknown land.

SLADES HILL - On a field nearby was a battery of anti-aircraft guns, during World War 11.

ST. MARY MAGDALENE CHURCH - The prominent stone spire is a useful landmark, on top of Windmill Hill. It was designed by William Butterfield and built between 1881-3. A windmill was situated opposite the church.

WINDMILL HILL - As the name suggests there have been windmills here from the 16th. century onwards. The last one built in the early 19th. century was working until 1887. In 1901 the sails were removed and in September 1904 it was demolished.

Entrance gate plaque - Cunard Crescent.

Crown & Horseshoes Inn, New River Loop, Enfield.

THE NEW RIVER IN ENFIELD - 8 MILES

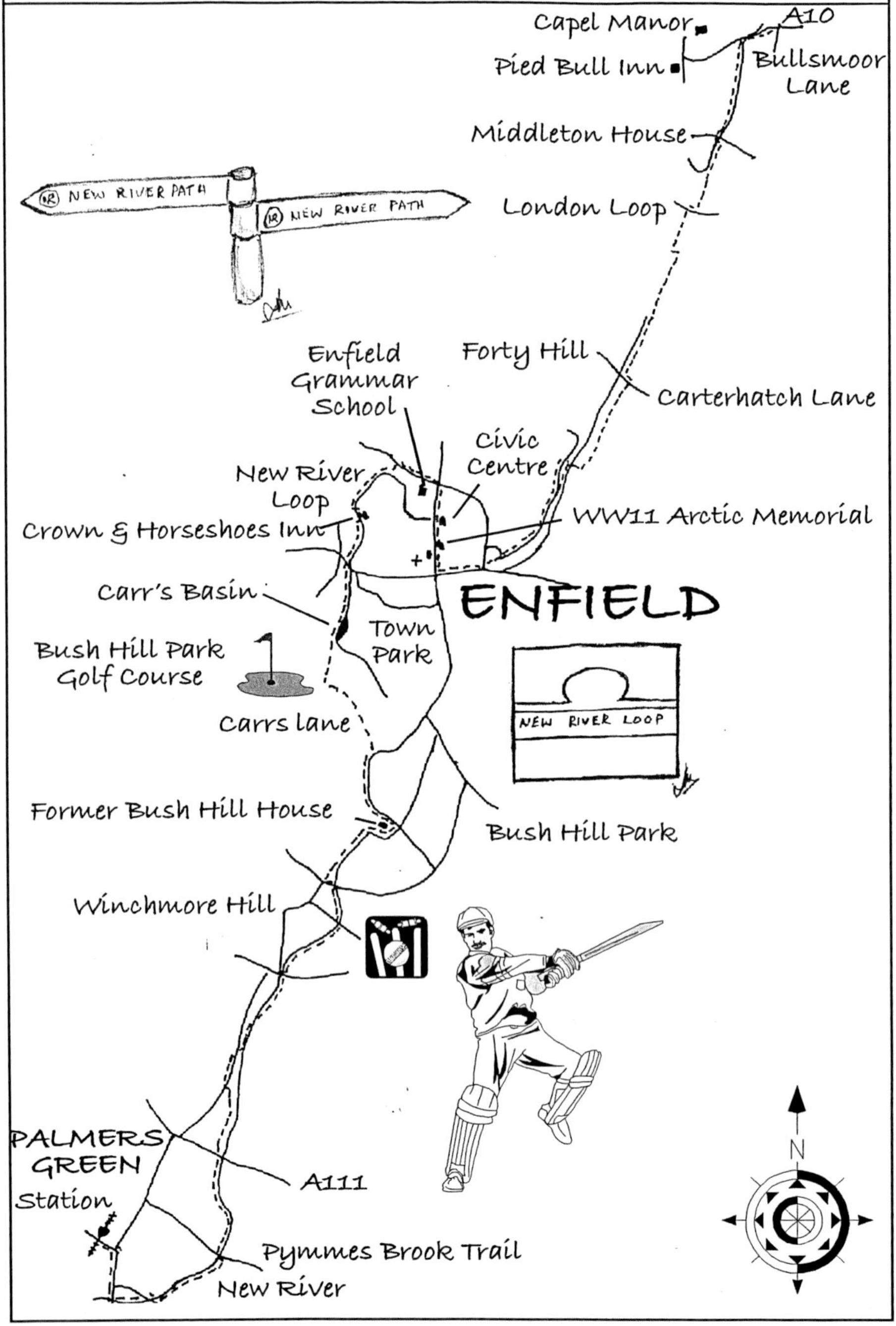

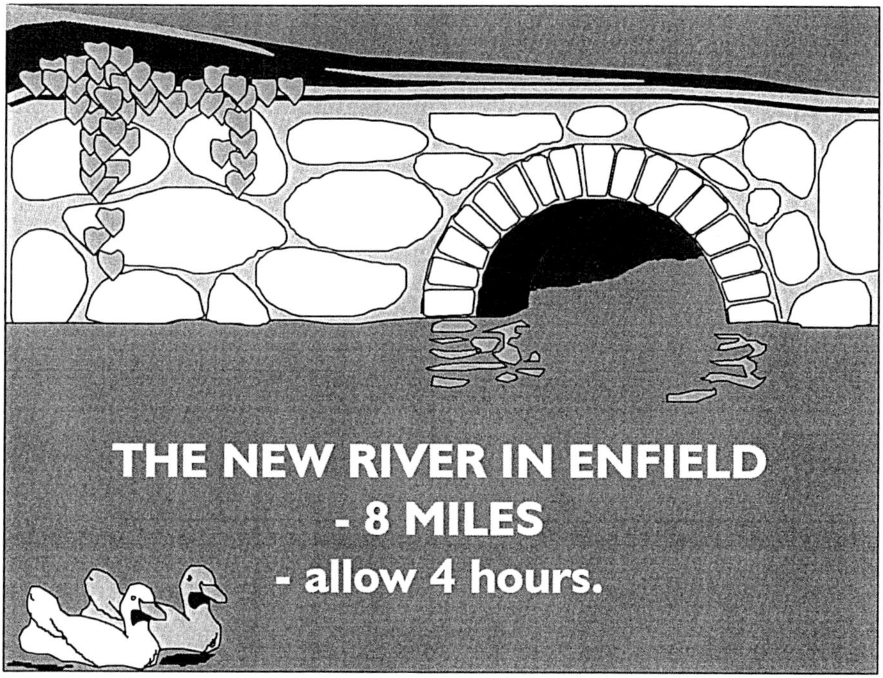

THE NEW RIVER IN ENFIELD
- 8 MILES
- allow 4 hours.

Basic route - Bullsmoor Lane - New River - Forty Hill - Enfield - New River Loop - Town Park - Carrs Lane - Bushey Hill - New River - Winchmore Hill - Pymmes Brook Trail - Palmers Green.

Map - O.S. 1:25,000 Explorer Series No. 173 - London North.

Start - Bullsmoor Lane, beside the A10. Reached via Bus No. 217 & 317.
End - Palmers Green Rail Station. Bus No. 121 or 329.

Inns - Crown & Horseshoes, River Walk, Enfield. The Stag Inn, Little Park Gardens, Enfield, just off the route. Orange Tree Inn, Winchmore Hill.

Cafe - just off the route in Church Street, Enfield.

ABOUT THE WALK - A walk along the New River in Enfield Borough from Bullsmore Lane in the north to Palmers Green in the south. The river is not only a remarkable 17th. century construction it is a tranquil haven in suburbia.

The walk is well signed by New River Path signs, and green metal kissing gates usually give access to the path beside it. At frequent intervals are history information boards, showing the route section and some local history. The path is well defined but does not always keep directly beside the river. Various parts are along an adjacent road, but usually paralleling it. As the river goes through pipes underground in Enfield Town, the route follows the New River Loop (Old Course) in the town. It is a fascinating walk, whatever the season.

WALKING INSTRUCTIONS - Starting from the bus stop before Bullsmoor Lane at the junction of the A10. Walk along the A10 to the crossroads and turn left along Bullsmoor Lane, with a sign for Pied Bull Inn - 200 yards off the route. You soon see the New River on your right and cross the bridge over it and turn left through the green kissing gate, beside a history board. Keep the river on your left and follow it to the next road, with Myddleton House to your right. Cross to your left to continue with the river on your right; beyond is a football field. A little further the New River used to turn for the Whitewebbs Loop, today it is taken through pipes here, keep straight ahead. On the right is an automatic weed clearing machine. Continue on the path by a metal fence and cross a footpath and onto the next one - The London Loop.

The river is still submerged and turn right then left to continue with it on your left. The river soon becomes open again on your left and reach a footbridge. Cross and continue now with the river on your right. Continue to a road with tower blocks on your right. Cross and keep the river on your right to the next road - Carterhatch Road. Turn left and descend to the first road on your right - Ladysmith Road. Turn right along it. Keep ahead into Lambourne Gardens and at house No. 172, turn right and follow the path which turns left to steps and regain the river, on your right. Cross a footbridge and follow the path to a road - Carnarvon Avenue. Follow this to its end to a footpath on the right. This leads to Willow Road. Turn left to the main road - A110 - Southbury Road. Turn right and now keep the New River Loop on your right - there are frequent plaques in the pavement showing your way. Keep ahead towards Enfield Town and at the main crossroads. Turn right along Silver Street. Soon pass on your right the former Church School of Industry and soon on your left the White Lodge - here a blue plaque records that Joseph Whitaker 1820-1895 lived and died here. He was the founder and publisher of Whitaker's Almanac. Opposite is the WW11 Arctic Campaign Memorail.

Continue along Silver Street and opposite the Enfield Civic Centre is a water filled section of the New River Loop. Soon after pass Enfield Grammar School and turn left along Parsonage Lane. Opposite Monastery Gardens, turn left rejoin the New River Loop. Follow the path right with the river on your left. Cross a footbridge and continue by the river on the right to the next footbridge bridge dated 1841, beside the Crown and Horseshoes Inn. Cross and turn left along River View, past houses in a delightful setting. After the last house keep straight ahead into a small park with history board and Millennium Fountain.

Cross Church Street with Trinity Church and Stag Inn on the left and take the second path on the righthand side of the New River Loop. Soon pass a large lake - Carr's Basin - and reach a footbridge over the loop. Leave the New River Loop and turn right over the bridge and up the tarmaced and fenced path ascending gently to a T junction. Turn left along Carrs Lane, mostly a footpath, as you pass Bush Hill Park Golf Course on your right. At the end reach the entrance to the golf club at Bush Hill. Turn right along the road and follow it as it curves left and becomes Bush Hill Road. In a short distance pass Cunard Crescent on your right with a blue plaque on the righthand gatepost - "Site of Bush Hill House" - where Sir Hugh Myddleton lived 1609-1613. The house was demolished in 1993. The name Cunard is after the founder of the Cunard line, who lived in the house in the mid 19th. century.

Just after go through a green kissing gate on the right and walk beside the New River on your left. Follow it round to steps and descend to Ridge Avenue. Turn left and walk along the road with the New River up on your left to the shops at Masons Corner.

Turn left and in a few yards right to a kissing gate and rejoin walking beside the New River. At the next road turn left and right to continue now with the river on your right. On you left is Winchmore Hill Cricket Club (1880). The field was pqart of the Ford Grove Estate. At first the club was known as the Winchmore Hill Village Cricket Club, but the word village was abandoned in 1912. According to a will of the owner in 1960, the club were granted a 99 year lease on the field, with an annual rent of one shilling (5p). The land to remain a recreation ground in perpetuity. For more details about the area see the book - *"A history of Winchmore Hill"* by S. Delvin. Regency Press, 1989.

Follow the path to a footbridge and cross the river and gain Fords Lane with shops to your right. Cross and bear half left along Farm Road and right again to rejoin the New River. At the next road with the Orange Tree Inn to your left, cross to your right and and keep the river on your left to Carpenters Gardens Road. Cross and continue with the river on your left. At the next road turn right to the main road, Greens Lanes, (A105). In a few yards turn left along River Avenue and follow this to the next road, Hedge Lane. Turn left to the next kissing gate and right to continue by the river on your left. Continue to another kissing gate and keep ahead with a park on the otherside of the river.

Follow the path to the next road and cross the river and turn right into Chimes Avenue. A few yards along here cross and a bridge and turn left to continue with the river on your right. Soon afterwards ascend steps and continue past a Mosque on your left. At the next road, Oakerthorpe Road, meet the Pymmes Brook Trail. Cross the road to the right and continue along the final section of the river, on this walk, on your left, to Greens Lane. Here leave the New River and turn right along the lane past Palmers Green Library on the left and on towards the main shopping area of Palmers Green. Turn left along Alderman's Hill to Palmers Green Rail Station and 121, 329 buses.

The New River Loop in Town Park.

Lilly Pond, Forty Hall - See London Loop Walk & Forty Hall walk.

Broomfield Park Lake - see Pymmes Brook Trail.

AROUND TRENT COUNTRY PARK - 4 MILES

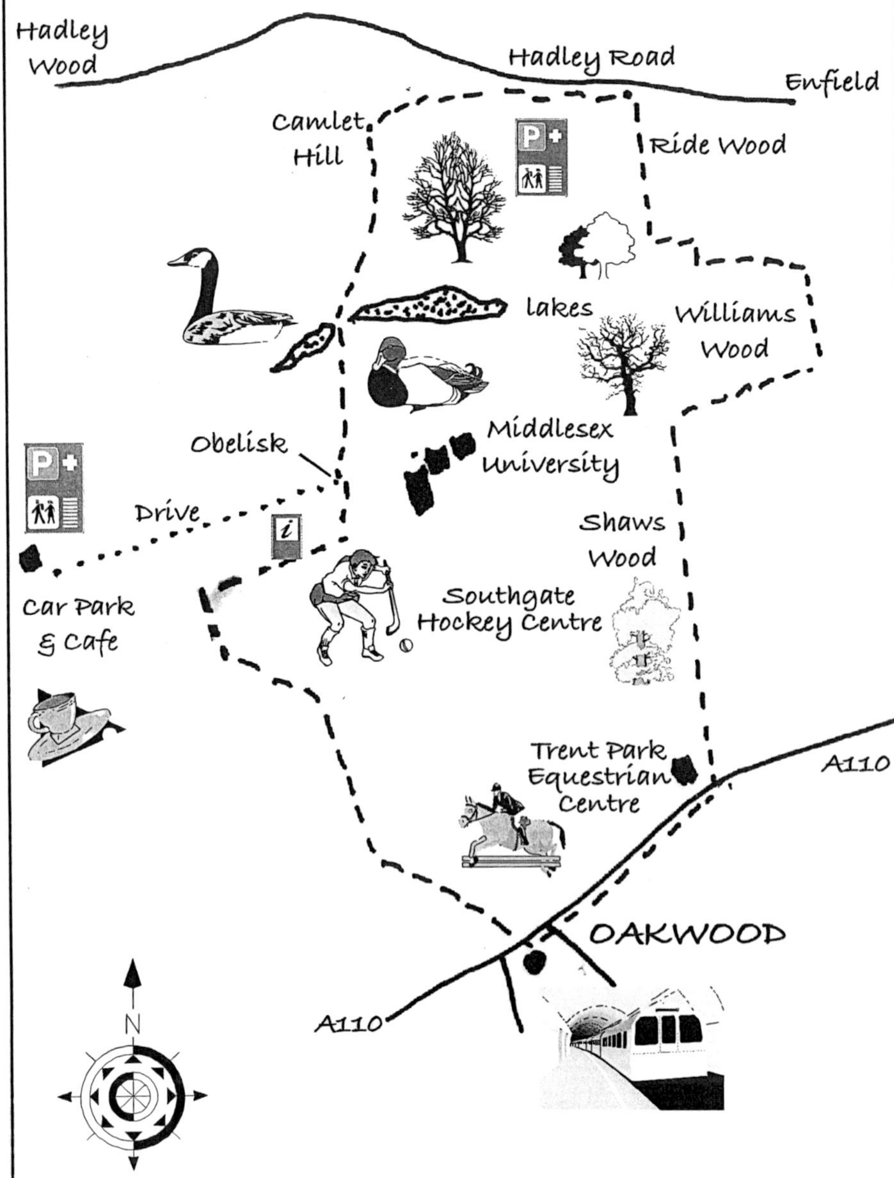

AROUND TRENT COUNTRY PARK - 4 MILES - allow 2 hours.

Basic route - Oakwood Underground Station - Trent Park - Southgate Hockey Centre - Ponds - London Loop - Camlet Hill - Hadley Road Car Park - Ride Wood - Williams Wood - Shaws Wood - A110 - Oakwood Underground Station.

Map - O.S. 1:25,000 Explorer Series No. 173 - London North.

Start and end - Oakwood Underground Station, Piccadilly Line. Also on Bus route 307 (Barnet). Alternative start using car parks - Off Cockfosters Road on the western side of the park. Hadley Road car park on the northern side.

Cafe - Park Cafe off the route near Cockfosters Road car park. Open 10.30 a.m. to 5.30 p.m.

ABOUT THE WALK - The principal aim of the walk is to walk around the park, clockwise, mostly in woodland. You see the main house and buildings of Middlesex University, cross the lakes and follow a fragment of the London Loop. If starting from the Cockfosters Road car park, simply follow the main drive to the visitor's Centre and obelisk in memory of Henry, Duke of Kent. Those starting from Hadley Road car park, the walk goes right past it.

WALKING INSTRUCTIONS - Opposite Oakwood Underground Station, turn right into Trent Country Park by path sign - Butterfly Meadows. The path keeps near the railway line on your left and after the first field enters pine woods. Still keep near the railway line along a fenced path and cross a small footbridge. Just after leaving the woodland behind, turn right onto a smaller path beside the righthand side of the field, by a tall hedge. Keep straight ahead soon having woodland on your left. At a junction of paths close to stream - Merryhills Brook, bear half left on a defined path with a stream bed and hedge on your left. Reaching woodland again and a solitary oak tree, bear right along an ascending track. Soon to your left can be seen the buildings and pitch of the Southgate Hockey Club.

At the top turn right, still in trees and soon reach the the buildings of the Hockey Club. Reaching the road here turn left past houses to a drive junction and obelisk on the left in memory of Henry, Duke of Kent. To your right is the main house of Middlesex University and to your left is the drive past the Visitor's Centre to the Cockfosters Road car park and Park Cafe. Ignore the second road on your right and cross onto a path beside a wooden fence on your left. Turn right along this path, passing College House to your right. Keep right with the fence on your right to a kissing gate as you descend in woodland. Continue ahead on the path to path junction and a kissing gate on the right. Don't go through, just keep straight ahead to pass between the lakes and follow the path as it curves right to a path cross roads. Here, briefly join the London Loop.

Continue ahead and now uphill on the wide track. Well up Camlet Hill take the first track on your right. Follow it past Hadley Road car park on your left. Where it curves left to Hadley Road, turn right past a white gate barrier and turn left onto a bridleway. Follow this along the northern edge of the park near Hadley Road to the far edge of the Ride Wood. Turn right, still on the bridleway, heading due south. Cross a footbridge over Leeging Beech Gutter and turn left, still on the bridleway, into Williams Wood which contains pine trees. Keep on the bridlepath near the woods perimeter as it turns right to the southern edge. Here turn right again with views southwards over Oakwood. Reaching the lefthand corner of the wood, turn left to continue on the bridlepath as you walk along the edge of Shaws Wood. Partway along the bridlepath turn left to continue on a footpath paralleling the bridlepath. Follow it to the A110 road and path sign. Turn right immediately passing the Trent Park Equestrian Centre on your right. Follow the road for less 1/2 mile to the shops of Oakwood on the left and underground station.

TRENT PARK COUNTRY PARK - Covers 413 acres. The mansion, now part of Middlesex University, was built in 1777 for Sir Richard Jebb. The last owner of the estate died suddenly in 1939, aged 50. As instructed in his will his ashes were scattered by the RAF over Trent Park. During World War I I, in 1942, the house was converted to a prison and an interrogation centre for important prisoners, including Rudolf Hess. 84 German Generals were held here and using hidden microphones, considerable information was obtained. After the war it became a teacher training college and in 1974 became Middlesex Polytechnic and later, Middlesex University.

The park has considerable woodland and is quite varied with oak, pine and hornbeam and smaller numbers of sweet chestnut, beech, holly, hazel and birch. For bird watchers the woodland offers opportunities to see nuthatch, tree creepers and wood peckers together with the more common birds of magpies, jays, blue tits, robins, wrens, blackbirds and dunnocks. While the lakes have Canada geese, mallard, tufted duck, moorhen, coot, pochard teal and widgeon.

For further details about Trent Park, see the book - "Trent Park - A short history to 1939" by Patrick Campbell. Published by Middlesex University Press 1997.

FORTY HALL, WHITEWEBBS PARK AND HILLY FIELDS PARK - 4 1/2 MILES

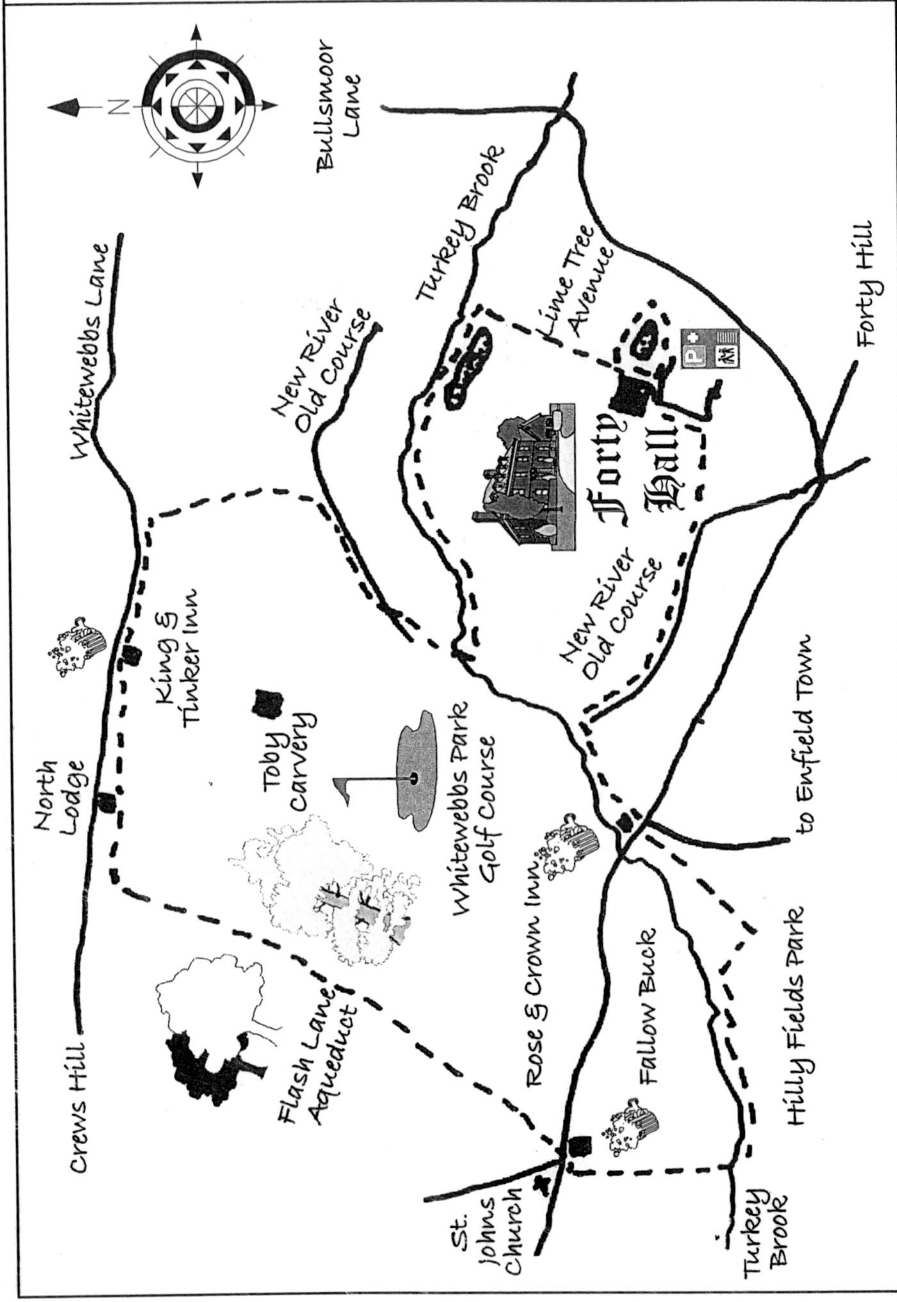

FORTY HALL, WHITEWEBBS PARK AND HILLY FIELDS PARK - 4 1/2 MILES - allow 2 to 3 hours.

Basic route - Forty Hall Car Park - Lime Tree Avenue - Turkey Brook - New River (Old Course) - Whitewebbs Lane - North Lodge - Whitewebbs Wood - Flash Lane Aqueduct - Flash Lane - Clay Hill - Hilly Fields Park - Rose & Crown Inn - New River (Old Course) - Forty Hall.

Map - O.S. 1:25,000 Explorer Series No. 173 - North London.

Car Park and start - Forty Hall. Alternative start at parking area near North Lodge on Whitewebbs Lane.

The nearest bus is the 191 (Brimsdown) which passes Forty Hill Roundabout. Here you can either walk upto Forty Hall or follow the path along the Old Course of the New River, to the signed path junction for Forty Hall.

Inns - King & Tinker, Whitewebbs Lane. ~~Fallow Buck~~, Clay Hill. Rose & Crown, Clay Hill.

EN2 9HA

Cafe - Courtyard Cafe, Forty Hall. Open 10.30 a.m. to 4.0 p.m.

ABOUT THE WALK - A really enjoyable walk, mostly in woodland, with much to see. You start from arguably Enfield's finest house, Forty Hall, and walk down the lime tree avenue past the site of Elsyng Palace to Turkey Brook and the London Loop. After passing ponds you soon head north and follow a small section of the old course of the New River, before gaining Whitewebbs Lane. Heading westwards you pass your first inn before descending southwards to the exposed Flash Lane Aqueduct. Ascending you reach your next inn The Fallow Buck at Clay Hill. Descending again you pick up the London Loop and Turkey Brook again as you walk through Holly Fields Park to your third and last inn, The Rose & Crown. Soon after you leave both the London Loop and Turkey Brook, and walk above a water filled section of the old course of the New River. Leaving it, you walk around the walled garden of Forty Hall and pond back to the car park. I took 9,583 strides on the walk!

WALKING INSTRUCTIONS - From the car park exit via the steps at the far lefthand side to the drive. Turn right and soon have the picturesque hall and pond on your left. Turn right at a kissing gate beside an information board about the former Royal Palace - Elsyng Palace. Bear slightly left and descend the double rowed Lime Tree Avenue, passing the site of Elsyng Palace. At the bottom keep ahead on a small defined path to Turkey Brook and the London Loop. Turn left on the wide path keeping the brook on your right. Soon pass a lily pond on your left and then a larger pond. Follow the path as it curves left to a footbridge and path sign - 1 1/4 mile footpath to Whitewebbs Lane. Turn right over the bridge and follow the path with a fence on your right - on your left is Whitewebbs Park Golf Course - and in five minutes reach a "gate" and a section of the old course of the New River - part of the Whitewebbs Loop. Walk beside it for awhile before following the path over it, to head northwards along a fenced path to Whitewebbs Lane.

Over the stile into a former lay-by turn left and in a few yards left then right to continue on a tarmaced path with a bridleway on the left. The path returns to the road and continue along it past the King and Tinker Inn. Soon after reach the drive into Whitewebbs (Toby Carvery) and cross a cattle grid. Immediately after turn right and follow the fenced bridleway along the northern side of the park. Reaching North Lodge, turn left then right, to continue on the bridleway to a lefthand corner, with Whitewebbs Lane immediately on the right. Turn left and descend this fenced bridleway in woodland and in 10 minutes reach Flash Lane Aqueduct on the left, with history board. Keep straight ahead with a small section of the old course of the New River on your left. Continue up the lane, now a track to pass Wildwoods Lodge and houses before reaching Clay Hill and the Fallow Buck Inn opposite - dates back 70 1734 and first recorded as the Fallow Buck Inn in 1761.

Cross and turn half right past the cattle trough placed here by the "Metropolitan Drinking Fountain and Cattle Trough Association". Behind is St. John's church. Walk a few strides along Strayfield Lane and turn left at the path sign and follow the tarmaced path into Hilly Fields Park, picking up another section of the London Loop. Pass a football pitch on your right and at the bottom cross a footbridge and turn left walking beside Turkey Brook. Follow the tarmaced path to the next bridge and turn half right and ascend the path to the top of the hill. Here turn left and follow the tarmaced path as it descends to Clay Hill, London Loop Section 17 notice board and the Rose & Crown Inn opposite. The Inn was known in 1716 and was visited by the notorious highwayman, Dick Turpin.

Cross to the immediate right of the inn and follow the path around the lefthand side of the field. Follow it as it curves right to another section of the old course of the New River, by path sign - Gough Park Walk. Turn right and follow the path with the water filled New River on your right. In less than 10 minutes reach another path sign on your left - Forty Hall - and gate. Here, leave the New River and follow this fenced path along the righthand side of the field with three solitary Wellingtonia trees in the middle. Follow the path to the walled garden wall of Forty Hall. Follow the path left beside to a gate on the right and enter the gardens - Coronation Gardens. Keep to the lefthand side to pass the Courtyard Cafe, and then the main hall, before reaching the pond. Bear right on the drive to return to the car park.

FORTY HALL - An exceptional Jacobean Grade I listed building, built for Sir Nicholas Rainton in 1629. He was a Haberdasher who amassed great wealth by importing cloth and silk from Italy. In London he held many important positions and in 1632 was the Lord Mayor of London. The hall, which has an interesting museum, and gardens are open to the public, free. His memorial can be seen in St. Andrew's church, Enfield.

For more deatils about the hall see the book - "Forty Hall" by Geoffrey Gillam. Published by the Enfield Archaeology Society, 1997.

CORONATION GARDENS - Opened by Her Royal Highness, the Princess Royal on 6th. October 2003.

ELSYNG PALACE - Now frequently dug by archaeologists, it w
Royal Palace to Henry 8th. and Elizabeth 1st. The name E
recorded in 1374 - Jordan de Elsyng and the Manor of E

KING & TINKER INN - Oldest inn in Enfield dating from the early 17th. century. According to the legend, James 1st. while out deer hunting on Enfield Chase, stopped alone at the inn for a drink. No one knew him as he had a quiet drink with a tinker. Later he revealed to the tinker who he was and knighted him; hence the inn's name.

FLASH LANE AQUEDUCT - part of the "Whitewebbs Loop" which was bypassed in 1850. The aqueduct was built in 1820 being cast by Hunter and English of Bow, London. The brickwork was by Henry Rogers and the total cost was £252 2 shillings. The 18 foot wide cast iron aqueduct was made in four sections and bolted and sealed together. Although overgrown and almost forgotten for more than a century, it has now been excavated to show its construction.

WHITEWEBBS PARK - Covers 196 acres, with parkland and extensive woodland. The present large white house was built in 1791 for Dr. Abraham Wilkinson. In 1931 it was sold to Enfield Council and became an old people's home. Today it is a Toby Carvery.

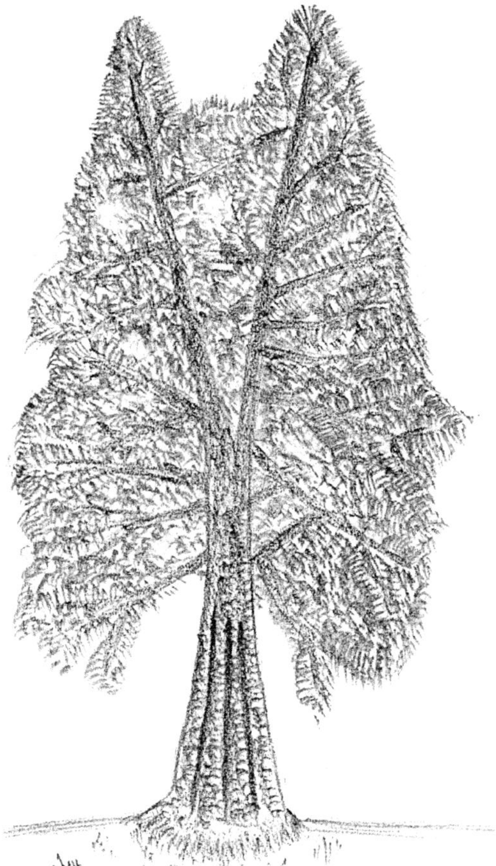

WELLINGTONIA TREES - (Sequoiadendron giganteum) trees, from the western side of the Sierra Nevada Mountains, (Sequoia National Park), California, USA. The tree was introduced into Britain in 1853. The English name, Wellingtonia, was given in honour of the Duke of Wellington (1769-1852). The American name is the Big or Mammoth Tree, and they are indeed the largest trees in the world. Some in the Sequoia National Park are big enough to drive a car through, and weigh over 1,000 tons and live for upto 3,000 years. The reddish-brown fibrous bark is soft and spongy and becomes thick and fluted with age. The trees are conical shape with a broad tapering trunk, with drooping branches. Both sexes of flowers are on the same tree - male are small yellow flowers and female pale green. The cones are one to two inches long and the pine needles when crushed have a minty smell.

GROVELANDS PARK - 2 MILES

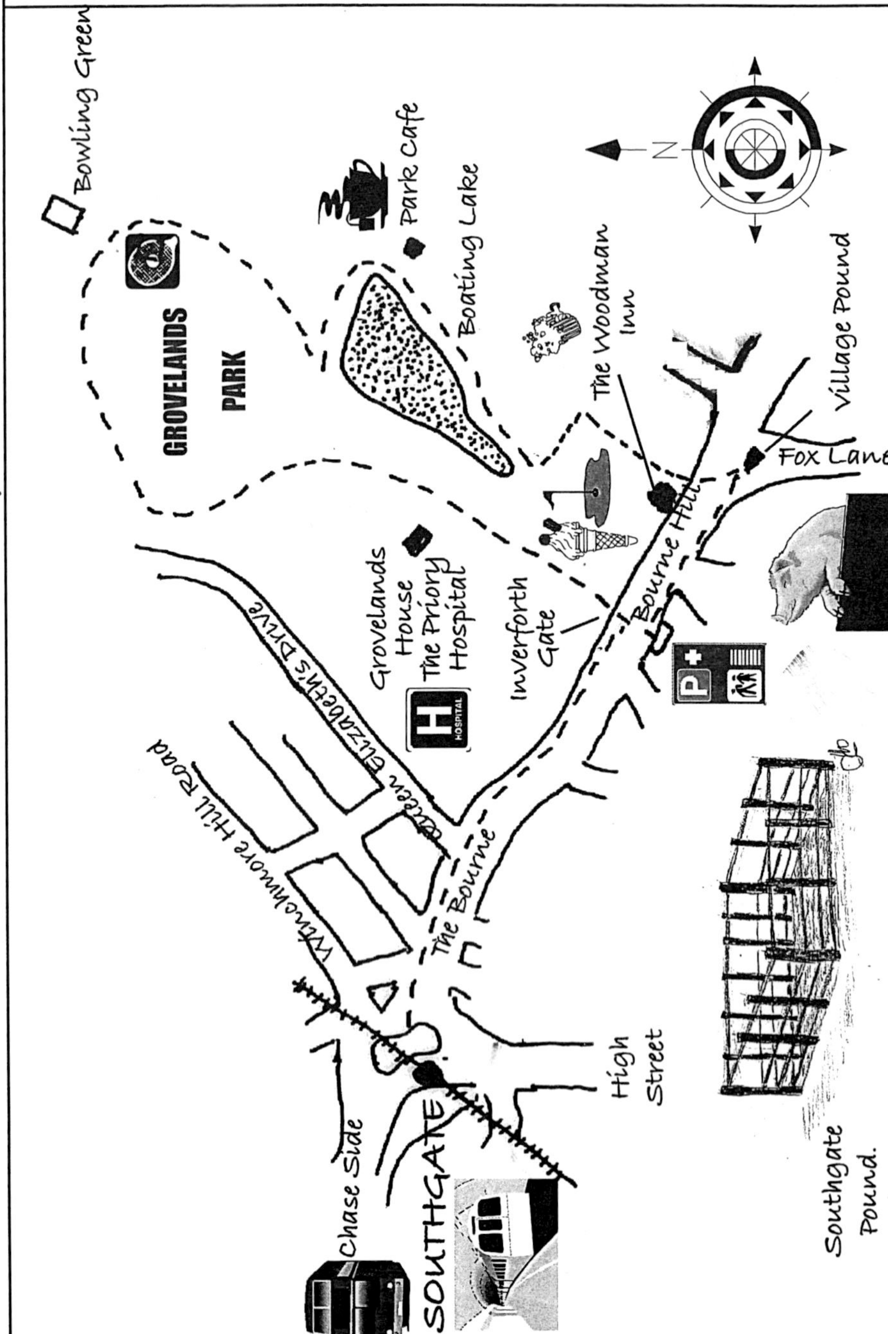

N14 6RD

Basic route - A circular walk around Grovelands Park, including a visit to the Village Pound.

Start - The walk can either be started from Southgate Underground or Bus Station - 2 mile walk. Or from the car park opposite the Inverforth Gate entrance to the park - 1 1/2 miles.

Maps - O.S. 1:25,000 Explorer Series No. 173 - London North. London A to Z Street Guide.

Inn - The Woodsman Inn, Bourne Hill.

Cafe - Park Cafe and ice-cream from Golf shop, near entrance.

ABOUT THE WALK - Grovelands Park is a particularly attractive and unspoilt park with extensive grass meadows, a large lake and woodland on the eastern side. You also pass Grovelands House, now The Priory (North London Hospital). Leaving the park you visit the historic Village Pound, before returning to the car park or Southgate.

WALKING INSTRUCTIONS - Starting from the Inverforth Gate entrance to the park - the car park is opposite. (If starting from Southgate Underground Station cross the main road at the round about and follow The Bourne road (A111). Enter the park and follow the tarmaced path, first past the small Golf course area on the right. Follow the path as it curves left past Grovelands House on your left. Later it reaches the northern perimeter of the park as it turns right and eventually passes the tennis courts on the right. Continue on the tarmaced path with a small intermittent stream on your left and woodland. Ascend the path to the righthand side of the lake and turn left onto another tarmaced path that keeps near the lake. Follow it right as it passes the Park Cafe and children's pay area on your left.

At the end of the lake, turn left onto a path with the golf course on your right. Ascend gently to the park's perimeter and tarmaced path. Turn right along it past the golf course and onto Bourne Hill. To your right is The Woodmans Inn, but first cross to your left to the wooden Village Pond. After your visit return to the inn's side of the road and descend to the Inverforth Gate and car park on the left. Those returning to Southgate, keep straight ahead along the road - The Bourne - back to Underground and Bus Station.

Grovelands House.

GROVELANDS HOUSE - Originally known as Southgate Grove, it was designed by John Nash and built between 1797-8 for Walker Gray, a wealthy London brandy merchant. The original estate of 230 acres was landscaped by Humphry Repton. The house became a Priory Hospital in 1985.

GROVELANDS PARK - Officially opened on Saturday April 12th. 1913, covering 60 acres.

For further details about the house and park, see the book - "The Story of Grovelands" by Matthew Eccleston.

SOUTHGATE VILLAGE POUND - This is a rare example[le of a wooden pound, which were a village feature in the 18th and 19th century. Here were kept stray farm animals and only on payment to the Pinner, were your animals released. The poundage was a fixed sum regardless of how many animals were in the pound. In the late 19th. century it was 1 shilling and 4 pence (7p). If the animals were in the pound for longer than 8 hours, a pail of water and hay was supplied at a charge of 8d (4p). The last time it was used in 1904 when a lost pig was impounded. The Pinner was Mr. Henry Reed, landlord of The Woodsman Inn - 1897 - 1904. The locals often joked that the landlord, "sold beer by the pound!" The historic site was restored in 2001. It is hard to imagine with all the surrounding suburbia, but this was once rural countryside!

THE WOODMAN INN - Originally two 18th. century cottages. Later made into one and the owner in 1868, a retired police sergeant, obtained a licence to serve ale.

SOUTHGATE STATION - Opened on March 13th. 1933. Cockfosters opened a few months later on July 31st. 1933.

WALKING THE STREETS OF EDMONTON - 5 MILES

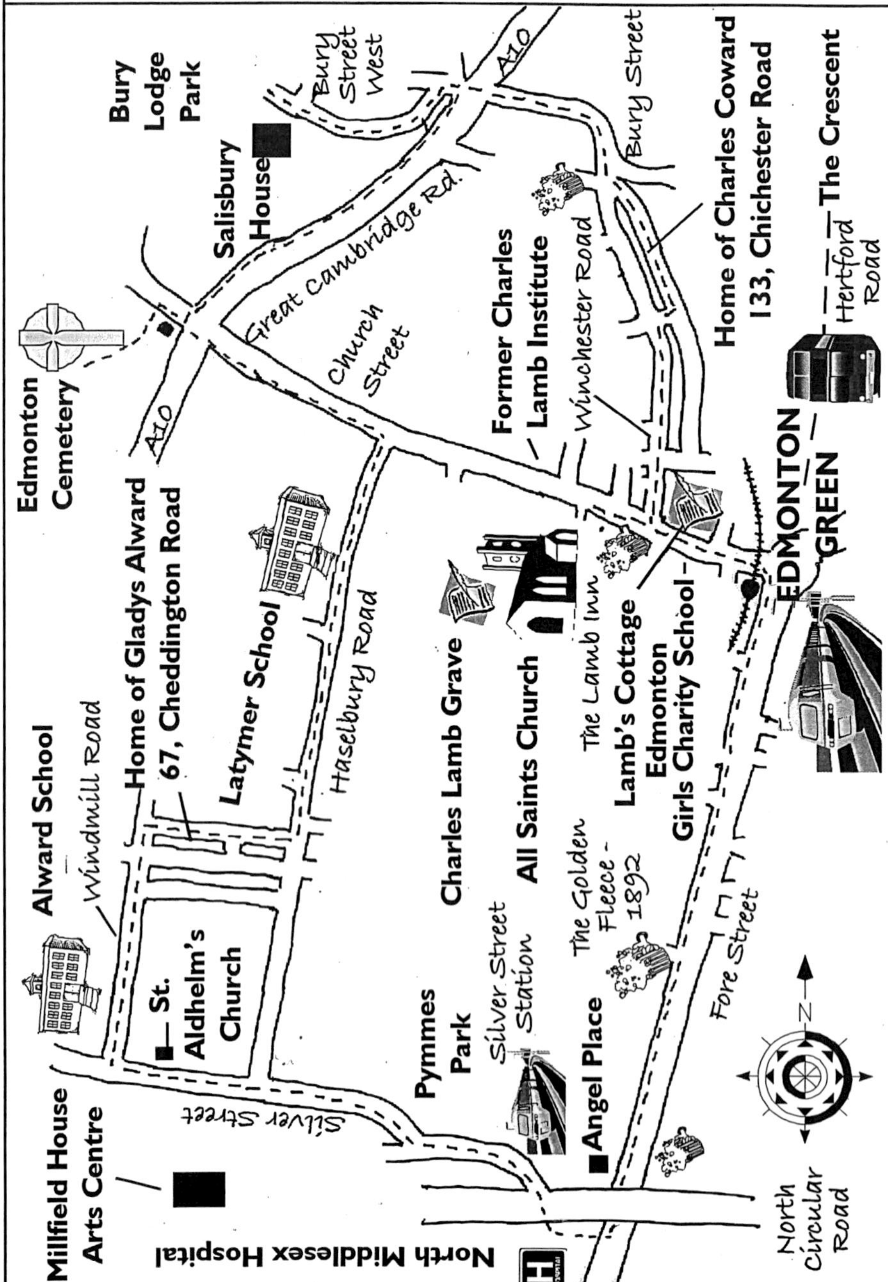

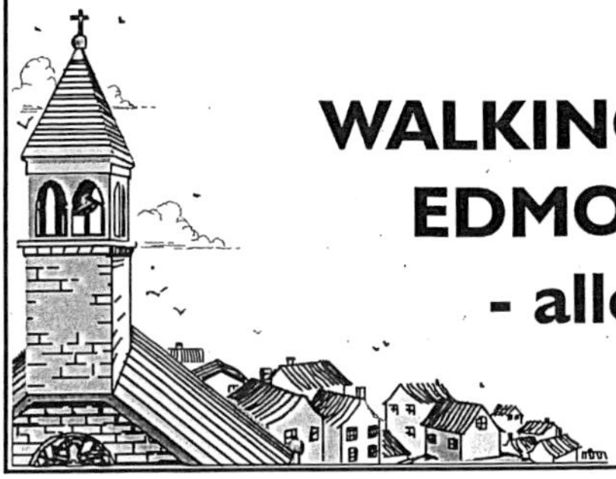

WALKING THE STREETS OF EDMONTON - 5 MILES - allow 2 to 3 hours

Starts and end - Edmonton Green Rail Station. The Bus Station is almost opposite.

Several cafe's and inns are along the walk, as detailed in the text.

ABOUT THE WALK - In 2006 a leaflet on the Edmonton Heritage Trail was published with detailed notes on the interesting story and development of this part of the London Borough of Enfield. Many of the places on this walk are included in this walk. On several houses can be seen the blue plaques describing where notable people once lived here. While many of the historical buildings has a circular green plaque detailing its name. This is a walk with a difference to see many historical buildings which are almost "hidden" by the surrounding shops and suburbia. In fact on my first walk I missed Lamb's Cottage on Church Street, as it was set back from the road; the others houses were close to the road. It is upto you how long you take to walk round for there is much more to see than can be written about here. You may want explore All Saints Church and graveyard more fully; or look at the many memorials in Edmonton Cemetery; or have a picnic in Pymmes Park on the way. Whatever you do, whether a local or not, I think you will be surprised and fascinated about the history lurking along the streets of Edmonton.

WALKING INSTRUCTIONS AND BRIEF HISTORY NOTES - Starting from Edmonton Green Railway Station - opened in 1872 -, opposite the war memorial, turn left along Church Street.

Almost immediately is your first blue plaque on No. 3 Keats Parade, Church Street to the poet John Keats. A cottage once stood here where he was an apprentice to Thomas Hammond, a local surgeon, between the years 1811-1815.

Continue along Church Street and in a few yards on your left is Edmonton's Girl's Charity School. Built in 1784, a girl in school uniform can be seen in a niche By public subscription £750 was raised and in 1784 Obodiah Legrew gave land near his house to build a school. The building cost 200 guineas (£210.00). The first schoolmistress had twelve children and earnt £12 per year. In 1793 there were 36 children and the schoolmistress's salary had more than doubled to £30 per annum. Each child was given annually a gown, petticoat and hat and every six months, new shoes and stockings. The school closed down in 1904.

A few yards later on the right is Lamb's Cottage. Dating to about 1800 this was Charles Lamb's (1775-1834) last home with his sister Mary (1764-1847). Charles Lamb is one of the finest 19th. century poet's and essayist. His most popular essay was, "Essays of Elia." Worked for the East India Company and enjoyed and wrote about both London life and countryside life. Their grave is in All Saints Churchyard.

Continuing on along Church Street, pass the Lamb Inn on the left, then Winchester Road on the right - your will be walking along here soon, but first continue along Church Street, passing Rosies Inn on the left before All Saints Church. Opposite is the Tower Gym, which was originally built in 1908 as the Charles Lamb Institute.

The Lamb Inn, Church Street, was originally the Viking Cafe. The inn opened on February 18th. 1993 after some £450,000 had been spent on it to convert to an inn.

Rosies - formerly the Rose & Crown Inn and one of the oldest in Edmonton, dating back to the late 17th. century. It was rebuilt in 1936 and at one time was known as the Rat & Carrot,

All Saints Church - There are Norman fragments in the south wall, but most the present church, including the tower is 15th. century. Inside are many monuments from the 16th to 19th. centuries. Beyond the church tower can be seen a railed gravestone area and here can be seen the tomb to Charles Lamb and his sister, Mary.

Return to Church Street and turn right along it retracing your steps to Winchester Road on the left. Turn left along here until you reach Glastonbury Road on the right. Turn right along here and in a few yards left along Chichester Road. At No. 133, on the left, is the blue plaque of the home of Charles

Girls Charity School, Church Street.

Coward (1905-1976). Although his surname would seem the opposite, he was no coward, for he rescued prisoners from Auschwitz. He lived here between 1945-1976. Continue along Chichester Road to its junction with Winchester Road beside the Rising Sun Inn. The original Rising Sun Inn, which was 350 years old, was pulled down in 1933. The license was transferred to this new inn.

Turn right and left to follow Bury Street to the A10 - Great Cambridge Road. Cross over and in a few yards left beside the shops of Cambridge Terrace, following Bury Street West. You will retrace your steps to near the shops. But first continue along the road to Salisbury House on the left, with Bury Lodge Park just beyond. The timber framed building with overhanging eaves dates back to the late 16th. century and is now an Arts Centre. Once about to be demolished, it has been restored in the 1980's. Inside is a 17th. century fireplace, a panelled room and wall paintings. The Edmonton Urban District Council bought the building in 1936 for £4,500.

Retrace your steps back along Bury Street West to the bend before the shops. Turn right on a path to the A10 and walk along its righthand side to the crossroads and traffic lights at Church Street. Cross and turn right and in a few yards left into Edmonton Cemetery. Walk through the archway and bear slightly left and in a few yards on your right can be seen the War Memorial and tombs to many serviceman. Opposite can seen the large tomb to the victims of the 1938, Dunholme Road Air Disaster. The cemetery opened in 1884 and has many fine memorials.

Retrace your steps back to the entrance and turn right and cross the A10 and walk along Church Street. After several roads on the right, turn right along Haselbury Road. Pass Latymer School on the right, founded in 1624. Latymer was a great benefactor to the school and upon his death he left property to the school, as well as helping eight poor boys from Edmonton. Pass Latymer Cafe on the left, before turning right along Cheddington Road. On your left at No. 67 can be seen the blue plaque to Gladys Aylward (1902-1970); a famous missionary to China. Turn left along Windmill Road and near its end and junction with Silver Street, on the right is Aylward School.

Turn left along Silver Street, with St. Aldhelm's Church on the left. An impressive example of Art Nouveau Gothic style built in 1903 and designed by William Douglas Caroe. Almost opposite on the right - and now on a fragment of the Pymmes Trail - turn right through the gates to se the Millfield House Arts Centre; the Millfields Theatre is well to your right. The house

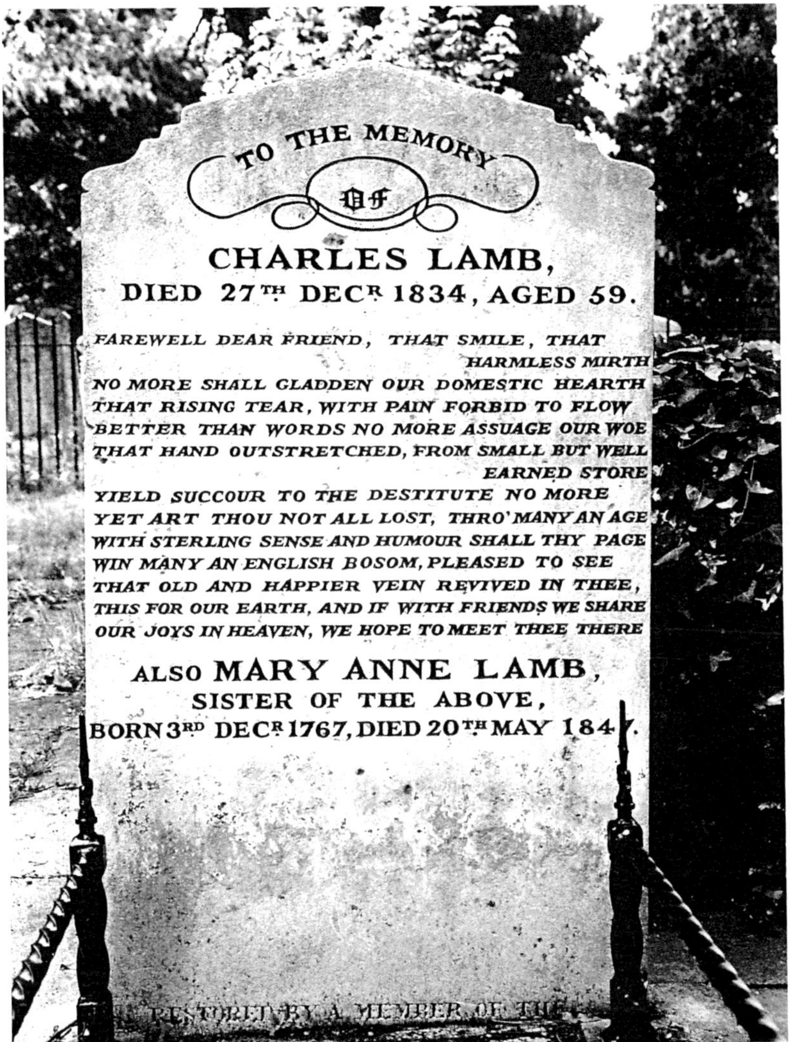

Charles and Mary Lamb gravestone in All Saints churchyard.

Lamb's Cottage Heritage Trail Plaque - a typical Edmonton Heritage Trail plaque

dates from the late 18th. century and was the home of Robert Mushet, who worked as a metallurgist at the Royal Mint. From 1849 to 1913 it was a workhouse school ran by the Strand Board of Governors. During World War I Belgian refugees were housed here. From 1917 to 1971 the building was used as a hospital for epileptics. Following its closure it was made into an arts Centre.

Return to the 19th. century Lodge, entrance gates, and Silver Street and turn right passing The Bull Inn and then Pymmes Park entrance on your left. The oldest park - 1899 - in Edmonton and formerly home to the Cecil family. The house was destroyed in the 1940's and the Tudor walled garden is all remains of this once important residence.

On your left is Silver Street Station. Continue to the North Circular Road and bear right to descend and cross through the subway. On the other side reach, on your right, the North Middlesex Hospital; part of which was originally the Edmonton Union Workhouse built in 1842.

Turn left beside the North Circular Road to the traffic lights and shops. Cross to your left to Fore Street. On the corner is Angel Place, a delightful Georgian terrace built about 1780. A blue plaque here records the site of the turnpikes roads here 1713 - 1826.

Continue along Fore Street, passing the Crown & Anchor Inn. Pass shops and on the left the Golden Fleece Inn, dated 1892. Soon after on your left is the former Central Library dated 1897.

Edmonton's most famous inn - The Bell Inn, Fore Street, was known in 1603, and was rebuilt three times, but was demolished in the 1960's. Once popular with Charles Lamb, it is the inn associated with the tale of John Gilpin and the galloping horse. His runaway horse dashed up the Lea Valley. William Cowper (1731-1800) wrote a famous poem about the incident - *"The Diverting History of John Gilpin."* Tells the story of how John Gilpin followed his wife and family on a borrowed horse, while they rode in a chaise and pair. When they reached the Bell Inn, Edmonton, his wife told him they had arrived. However the horse knew there was ten miles to go to Ware, where John Gilpin had a house. *(The John Gilpin Inn at Ware, shows him on horseback with his wig flying!)*

> *"For why? His owner had a house*
> *full ten miles off at Ware."*

The story was first published in the Public Advertiser in 1782.

Lamb's Cottage, Church Street.

Salisbury House, Bury Street West.

Continue along Fore Street back to Edmonton Green Rail Station. The bus station is further ahead on the right, as is the main shopping complex. If you walk a little further along Hertford Road, you will come to Edmonton's finest terrace - The Crescent. Built in the 1820's it is a magnificent sweep of buildings, reminiscent of Bath, with the pediment off centre; this was because it was later extended at either end. Return back, the same way, to the bus station or rail station.

The Crescent Pediment, Hertford Road.

The Dunholme Road Aeroplane Disaster - September 4th. 1938

"The worst plane disaster of its kind this country has ever known, took place at Edmonton early on Sunday afternoon."

Thirteen dead, 15 injured - seven seriously.

The pilot, Sergeant S. R. Morris, in his early twenties, of the No. 1 Elementary and Reserve Flying Training School, took off from Hatfield Airfield, in a two seater Hawker Audax. He was told to practise taking off, landing and climbing turns, close to the airfield; basically within three miles. He was flying solo with ballast in the second seat. For unknown reasons the pilot flew to Edmonton, 13 miles away. There, from a height of 1,000 feet he put the plane in a dive and pulled out low above the houses. He flew over Pymmes Park where a Scout Jamboree was taking place, and waved. Keeping low he let the nose drop and in doing so the undercarriage hit the roof of a house at the corner of Dunholme Road, at 2.40 p.m. The plane then bounced across the road and crashed into no. 28 and the torn off engine ending up in the porch of No. 30. Many people rushed out and two brothers, James Letch (24) and Edward Letch (20) from house no. 21 and John Euseden tried to rescue the pilot. But, within moments the seeping petrol from the ruptured fuel tanks blew up killing them and others, and setting houses ablaze.

Ambulances and the fire brigade were soon on hand and the injured were taken to the County Hospital.

The RAF arrived at 10.0 a.m. the following day to remove the wreckage and within 45 minutes it was loaded and on its way from the site.

The reports afterward confirmed that there was good visibility - 12 miles and the cloud base was at 5,000 feet. The plane was in good mechanical order, and had already been used for 2 1/2 hours that morning.

The Council Houses were assessed for damage and house no. 28 was the worst damaged with five others needing repair. The initial estimate was £997. 0s. 0d.

The Mayor quickly established a fund which grew over the subsequent weeks to over £3,000.

On the following Friday, after the disaster, the funerals were held, with an estimated 20,000 people lining the streets as the cortege passed by. The eleven victims - another died later from injuries and the pilot was cremated elsewhere - were buried in four family graves in Edmonton Cemetery and can be seen today - The Saunders family, husband and wife and their two children; The Letch brothers and James Tant, aged 8, who was playing outside in the road when the plane hit; John Euesden, who died trying to help others, and his wife Lilly who died years later; and the Callaghan family, the mother and her three children.

The disaster happened before the onset of World War Two and was at the time a major story. Detailed accounts with photographs appeared in the newspapers including the Daily Mirror - September 5th. 1938 and in the Tottenham & Edmonton Weekly Herald. The latter continued the story over subsequent weeks. A full description of the events and measures taken was recorded in the Edmonton Council Minutes in 1938. Today there is nothing to be seen at Dunholme Road. The makers plaque of the plane is believed to be in the reserve stock of Forty Hall Museum. 2008 is the 70th. anniversary. Apart from the grave in Edmonton Cemetery, the Letch brothers and John Euesden are recorded on the Roll of Honour board in Edmonton Library.

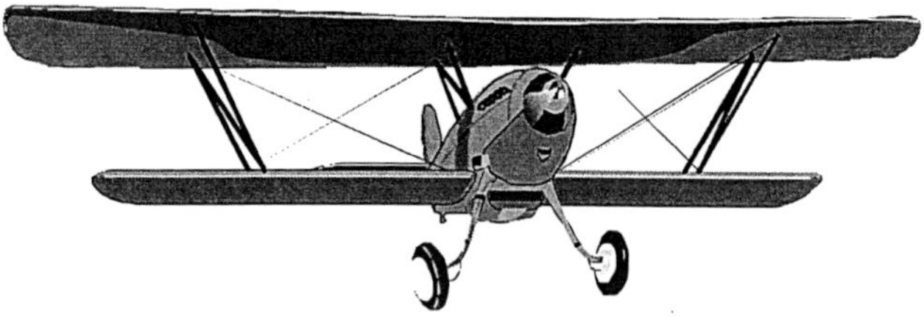

Hawker Audax (the above graphic is of a biplane, similar to a Hawker Audax), was an Army Co-Operation aircraft. More than 625 were built with the first one flown on December 29th. 1931. Production continued to 1937 and many of the planes saw active duty during World War I I.

PLANE SPECIFICATIONS -
WINGSPAN - 37 FEET 3 INCHES
LENGTH - 29 FEET 7 INCHES
HEIGHT - 10 FEET 7 INCHES.
ENGINE - ROLLS-ROYCE KESTREL IB; 530 H.P.
MAX. SPEED - 170 M.P.H. AT 2,400 FEET.
CEILING - 21,500 FEET
ENDURANCE - 3 HOURS 30 MINUTES
ARMAMENTS - TWO 0.303 IN. MACHINE GUNS, ONE FORWARD FIRING AND ONE IN AFT COCKPIT.
BOMB LOAD - FOUR 20 LB BOMBS OR TWO 112 LB SUPPLY CONTAINERS UNDER WINGS

THE DUNHOLME ROAD AEROPLANE DISASTER 1938

Central part of the memorial in Edmonton Cemetery.

James Letch 21, Dunholme Road
Edward Letch 21, Dunholme Road
John Euesden 5, Hawthorne Way

Lost their lives
whilst endevouring to rescue
the victims and pilot of the aeroplane
in connection with the
Air Disaster
at the Hyde Estate
on Sunday 4th. September 1938

Taken from the Roll of Honour board in Edmonton Library.

THE PYMMES BROOK TRAIL - 10 MILES

Map One - COCKFOSTERS TO BROOMFIELD PARK - 5 MILES

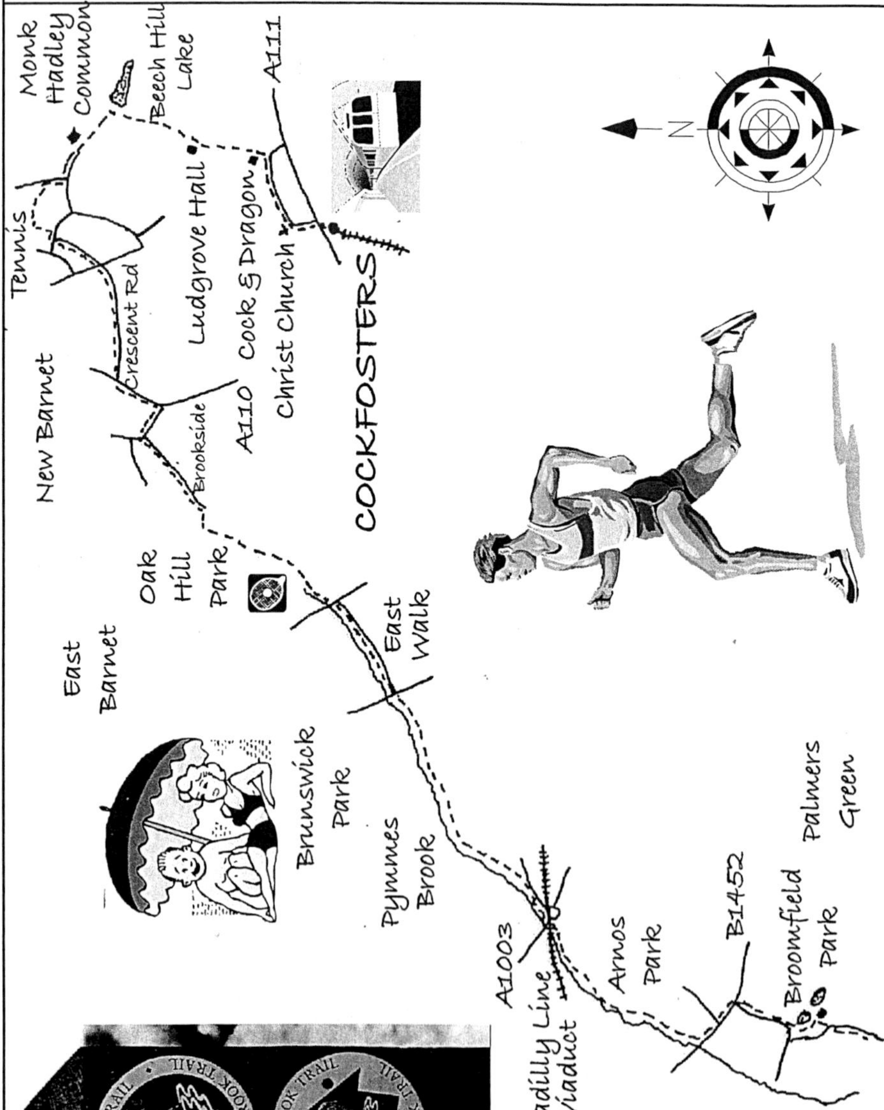

Pymmes Brook T

Back in the 1990s, a much-missed organisation called the London Walking Forum encouraged boroughs around London to come up with ideas for new walking routes. Sadly, the Forum no longer exists, leaving a cavernous hole in the promotion of walking in the capital, and many of the routes that were developed then have sunk into obscurity.

But one of them, the Pymmes Brook Trail, is to be relaunched in October. Created as a combined initiative of the London Boroughs of Barnet and Enfield, it originally ran for 10 miles across north-east London from Cockfosters station to Picketts Lock on the Lee Navigation, and naturally followed as closely as possible Pymmes Brook, a tributary of the River Lea.

The relaunch is accompanied by

Fountain Pond on Hadley Green Photo: Colin Saunders

a new and c
112-page guide
Colin Saunders,
Capital Ring, Lc
Downs Way and
familiar to many
describes a more l
that starts at Ha
the headwaters
rise, near the si
Barnet, one of th
and descends g
Barnet, Osidge,
Edmonton to fi
Hale, where the b
River Lea.

The route is su
such an urban ar
Monken Hadley
Hill Park, Bruns
Park, Broomfie
Meadow, Millfie
and Tottenham
advantage of seve
stretches that l
accessible in rece
London's least w
spots, Jack's Lake,
route, which also

lker

No. 103 September 2018

nblers pull s for first rk City week

SOUTH EAST

wa

London Ran
out the stop
National Pa

'rail relaunched

.rfully-illustrated the route by ›se guides to the ›n Loop, North nguard Way are blers. The book :al 13-mile route y Green, where Pymmes Brook ›f the Battle of 'ars of the Roses, y through East ners Green and at Tottenham k flows into the

isingly green in passing through Common, Oak :k Park, Arnos Park, Bowes Pymmes Park 1arshes, taking new brookside e been made years. One of -known beauty :ures early in the ses many places of historical and cultural interest, all described in the book.

Links with stations at High Barnet, New Barnet, Cockfosters, Arnos Grove, Palmers Green, Silver Street, Northumberland Park and Tottenham Hale, together with excellent bus connections, allow walkers to split the route into as many sections as they want, and there are many opportunities for refreshment.

The relaunch will take place over the weekend of 27 - 28 October, with a walk of about 6.5 miles each day. The Saturday walk, led by Dave Cockle of The Enfield Society, will start from High Barnet station at 10am and finish at Arnos Grove station. The Sunday walk, led by Colin Saunders, author of the guidebook, will start from Arnos Grove station at 10.30am and finish at Tottenham Hale station. There will be opportunities for refreshment at a cafe during the walks, but you can bring a picnic if you prefer, and there are pubs near the finish for further refreshment if required.

The book's RRP is £8.99, but South East Walker readers can buy a copy for the special price of £7.00 plus £2.00 p&p, from Colin Saunders at 35 Gerrards Close, London N14 4RH, or from his website www.colinsaunders.org.uk. Copies will be available on the walks. All profits will go to The Enfield Society.

The new guide.

THE PYMMES BROOK TRAIL - 10 MILES - allow 4 to 5 hours.

Basic Route - Cockfosters Underground Station - Monken Hadley Common - Beech Hill Lake - New Barnet - East Barnet - Oak Hill Park - Pymmes Brook - Brunswick Park - Arnos park - Broomfield Park - Edmonton - Pymmes Park - Salmon Brook - Pickett's Lock (River Lee Navigation).

Map - O.S. 1:25,000 Explorer Series No. 173 - London North.

Start - Cockfosters Underground Station - End of Piccadilly Line.
End - Pickett's Lock Leisure Centre for Bus (W8), back to Enfield and beyond.

Inns - The Drum Inn, East Barnet. The Golden Fleece Inn (1892), Edmonton Green. The Cart Overthrown Inn, Pickett's Lock Lane.

Cafe - Park Cafe, Oak Hill Park - off the route. A1 Cafe & Kebab, soon after Salmon Brook on lefthand side of B137 (Montagu Road).

ABOUT THE WALK - An absolutely delightful walk, along a well signed trail; infact I like it so much I have walked three times in the last six months - twice in the rain and once in blistering sun! As I like to walk nearer twenty miles a day it is not long enough. But as I live on the Enfield side of Waltham Cross, I walk home via the River Lee Navigation to Enfield Lock and on; adding another 6 miles - see separate walk!

More than half the trail is within the London Borough of Enfield with the rest being in the London Borough of Barnet. It would be a shame not to walk it all for it passes through several delightful parks where the Pymmes Brook flows. We owe much gratitude to the two borough's for creating this walk, which is well signed by blue and white logo of stream and weeping willow tree.

From Cockfosters you soon enter woodland of Monken Hadley Common, which is also part of the London Loop Walk - see separate section. Turning south easterly the trail enters Oak Hill Park, then Brunswick Park with the Pymmes Brook trickling through. Next it is into Arnos Park and the Piccadilly Viaduct before gaining Broomfield Park and now in Enfield Borough. Soon after, you cross the New River and pass several of the historical buildings of Edmonton before walking through Pymmes Park. A brief road walk brings you to the Salmons River and the final road walk to Pickett's Lock and the tranquil River Lee Navigation. Here you have to retrace your steps to reach the Leisure Centre and transport home. Almost all the trail is along tarmaced paths, beside roads and through the parks.

WALKING INSTRUCTIONS - Starting from Cockfosters Underground Station, cross the road to the right to Chalk Hill. Walk along the road and soon pass your first Pymmes Brook Trail sign. At the corner with Christ Church, follow the road road right and take the third road on your left - Games Road. Immediately pass the Cock & Dragon Inn on your left. On your right is the start of the woodland of Monken Hadley Common. Follow the road round to the right to Ludgrove Hall on the left. Here reach a track and enter the woodland descending to a footbridge and up to your right is Beech Hill Lake. Keep ahead a few more yards before turning left, as Pymmes Brook Trail signed, through a kissing gate. Follow the path to Baring Road with Livingstone School on the right. Follow the road and take the first road on your right - Lawton Road. Partway up and opposite house No. 6, turn left into a small park. Walk beside the tennis courts on the left to a water fountain and turn left to reach Park Road. Turn right and in a short distance left along Crescent Road. Keep straight ahead along this road for 1/2 mile to Brookhill Road (A110), with Brookhill Nursery opposite. Turn left and pass the shops of Pymmes Parade and soon after right down Cat Hill and into East Barnet.

Just before The Drum Inn, at the bottom, turn left along Brookside, with

Beech Hill Lake.

houses on your left and parkland and stream on your right. Follow the road to near its end and turn right down steps and on towards a footbridge. Don't cross, turn left and follow the tarmaced path close to Pymmes Brook on your right, as you walk through Oak Hill Park. As you walk along you will see how the trail's logo was conceived by the flowing brook and weeping willow trees. Pass a football pavilion on the right and then tennis courts - the path to your right here leads to the Park Cafe. Keep straight ahead and out of the park. Cross the road and continue in parkland on the right of the road - East Walk. Follow this to the next main road. Turn left then right opposite house no. 132 and enter Brunswick Park - Arnos Grove 1 mile. The tarmaced path is close to Pymmes Brook and is known as the Waterfall Walk. Follow the tarmaced path near the brook for nearly a mile to the Piccadilly Line viaduct and A1003 road.

Turn right and left and enter Arnos Park. Pass the viaduct on your right and flowing Pymmes Brook. Ignore all other paths and simply keep straight ahead as the tarmaced path keeps to the righthand side of the park, near the brook on your right. In little over 1/2 mile reach the B1452 road - Wilmer Way. Turn left and ascend slightly and at the second roundabout turn right - Powys Lane. Here go through a gate into Brookfield Park. Keep to the righthand path to the bottom pond and immediately past it, turn left. At the start of the next pond turn right to pass the covered Brookfield House and toilets on the right, and onto the entrance gateway. Walk through and keep straight ahead along

THE PYMMES BROOK TRAIL - 10 MILES - *Map Two* - BROOMFIELD PARK TO PICKETTS LOCK - 5 MILES

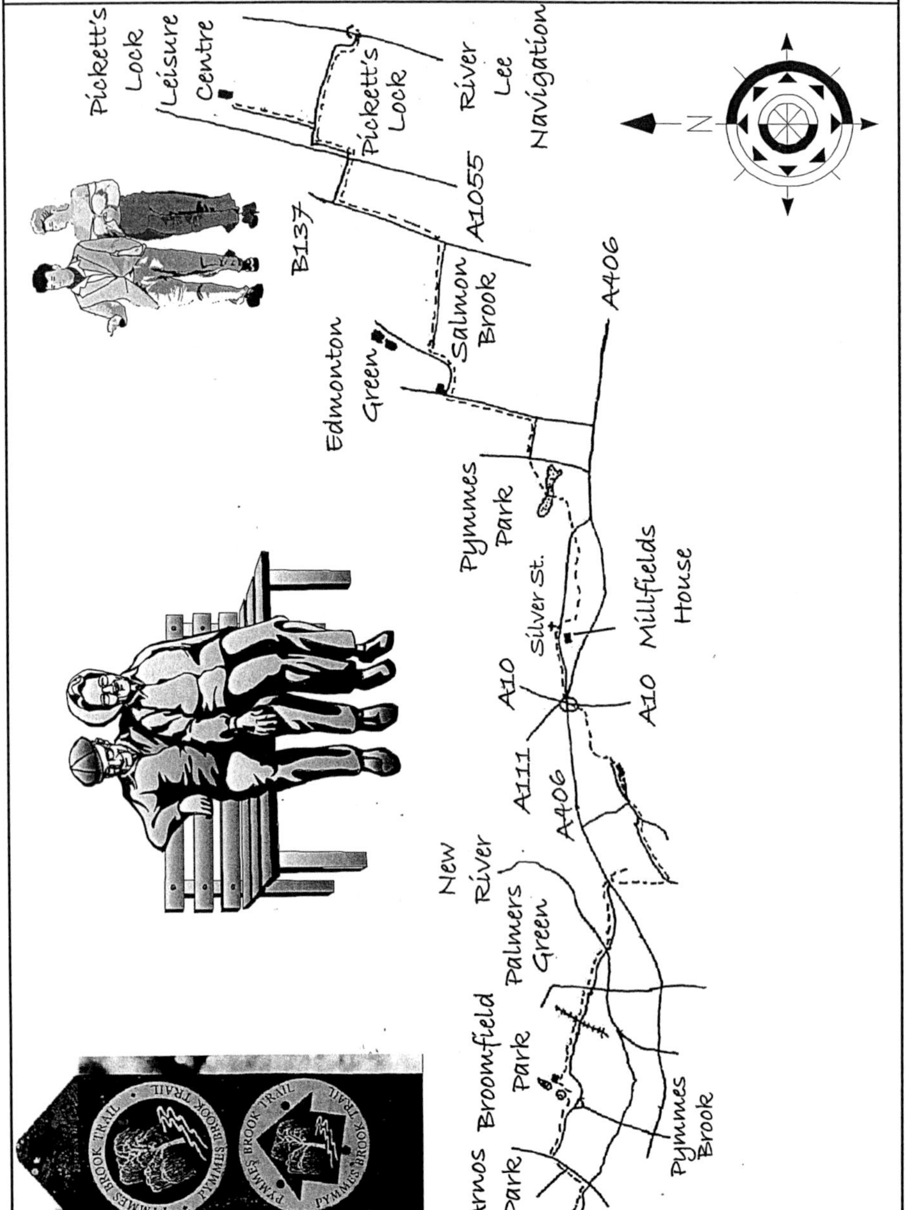

Oak Hill Park and the Pymmes Brook.

Broomfield Lane. Cross the railway line and pass Palmers Green Library on the right, before reaching the A105 road. Go straight across and walk along Oakthorpe Road. Cross the New River and pass a Mosque on your left.

Continue along the road to a Jet petrol Station on your left before the North Circular Road - A406. Turn right then left to cross the road via the pedestrian lights. Across turn left and then right along a tarmaced path by houses on the right. Follow it to Princes Avenue and turn left along it. Follow it to a T junction and turn left to a roundabout and shops. Cross and keep ahead along Tile Kiln Lane. passing Oakthorpe Primary School on your right. Soon after bear left to a gate and follow the tarmaced path to another gate and A10/A406 roundabout. Bear left and descend steps. Pass under the road and cross to your right to pass under another, before emerging on Silver Street and shops on the left.

Keep ahead along Silver Street passing Gladys Aylward School on the left and then St. Adhelm's church. Turn right here and pass Millfield Lodge and on towards Millfield House. Follow the drive to the house (Arts Centre) and then right through the gardens to the brook. Turn left beside it to a footbridge. Cross and follow the path on the left of the brook to Statham Grove. Keep

Arnos Park, the Pymmes Brook and Piccadilly Line Viaduct.

ahead along it past the Tanners End Free Church. Cross the road just after and continue ahead beside the brook on your left to Silver Street. (If this section seems difficult you can always walk along Silver Street.) Cross Silver Street into Pymmes Park. Walk past tennis courts on the left and then across the bridge between the two ponds. Bear half right to follow the tarmaced path past the children's play area to the toilets and onto the road. Go straight across and walk along Park Road to the A1010 road. Turn left and pass the Golden Fleece Inn, dated 1892. Continue towards Edmonton Green and immediately before the Police Station on the right, turn right along Plevna Road - named after a town in Bulgaria, which was under siege during the Battle for Independence from Turkey in the 1870's.

Follow the road round to your left and turn right along the path beside Salmons Brook. At the end turn left along the B137 - Montagu Road. Pass the AI Cafe on your left and infront of the The Cart Overthrown Inn, turn right along Pickett's Lock Lane. Follow it over the railway line and left beside the A1055 road. At the bottom, turn right, still on Pickett's Lock Lane. A short way along here on the left is the entrance to Pickett's Lock Leisure Centre and bus terminus (W8). But first continue along the lane and follow it round to your right. Just after turn left beside Burdens and onto Pickett's Lock No. 15 on the River Lee Navigation. Retrace our steps back to the leisure centre road on your right and ascend slightly to the complex and bus stop.

OAK HILL PARK - Once part of Hertfordshire and owned by St. Albans Abbey. Oak trees from here was used in the construction of the abbey. Became a park of Enfield Borough Council in 1930.

ARNOS PARK - Covers 43 acres and bought in 1928 for £22,762.

BROOMFIELD PARK - The historic Grade 11 listed house was badly damaged by fire in 1984. Since then it has been covered with plans to restore it. The park was bought for £25,250 and opened to the public on April 25th. 1903.

PYMMES PARK - Opened to the public in 1906. Originally a Tudor mansion and park, where in 1589 Robert Cecil, who later became the 1st. Earl of Salisbury, spent his honeymoon. The house has now gone being bombed during World War 11.

CART OVERTHROWN INN - Originally addressed as Marshside. The surrounding area was marshland with a rough track, which resulted in many carts being tipped over. The orginal inn dates back to 1752 and was first known as The Overturned Cart. In 1855 it was rebuilt and became known as the Cart Overthrown. The present inn was built in 1937.

PICKETT'S LOCK LEISURE COMPLEX - Officially opened by HRH the Duke of Edinburgh on June 13th. 1975. The tall granite stone, near the bus stop, recording this event was formerly a key stone in London Bridge - 1831-1968.

THE LONDON LOOP - 10 MILES
- *Map One* - COCKFOSTERS TO FORTY HALL

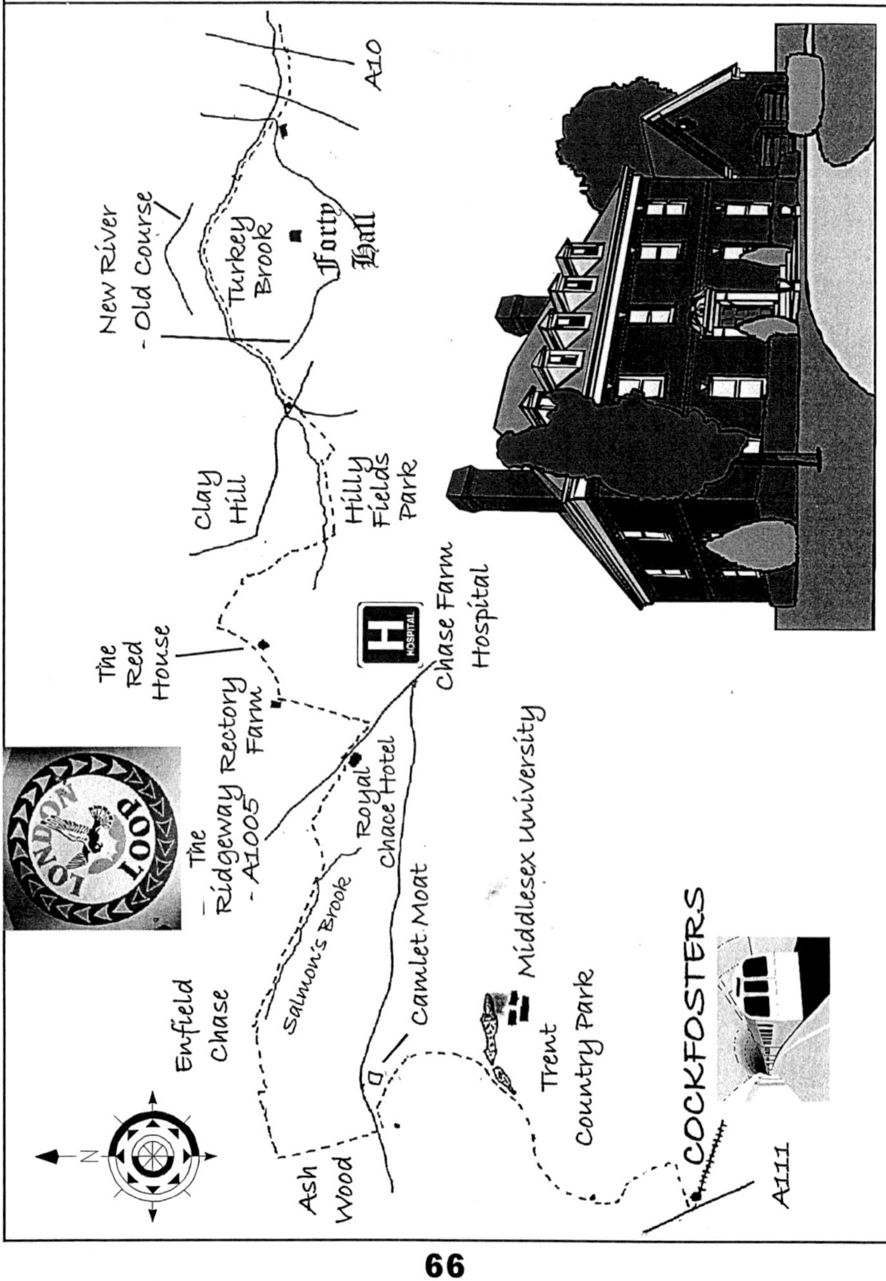

THE LONDON LOOP IN ENFIELD - COCKFOSTERS TO ENFIELD LOCK - 10 MILES - allow 4 to 5 hours.

Basic route - Cockfosters Underground Station - Church Wood - Oak Wood - Trent Country Park - Camlet Hill & Moat - Hadley Road - Ash Wood - Salmon's Brook - Enfield Chase - Enfield Chace Hotel - Rectory Farm - The Red House - Hilly Fields Park - Turkey Brook - Forty Hall Park - New River - A10 - Turkey Street - Enfield Wash - Albany Park - Enfield Lock.

Map - O.S. 1:25,000 Explorer Series No. 173 - London North.

Start - Cockfosters Underground Station - End of the Piccadilly Line.
End - Enfield Lock Railway Station.

Inns - Fallow Buck Inn, Strayfield Lane - just off the route. Rose & Crown, beside Hilly Fields Park. The Turkey Inn, Turkey Street, Enfield Wash. Tommy's Bar, Enfield Wash. The Greyhound Inn, Enfield Lock.

Cafe - Trent Park Cafe. Enfield Wash.

ABOUT THE WALK - The London Loop is a rewarding and surprising walk of some 150 miles around the outskirts of London. This is part of Section 17 and amply displays the walking variety to be found on the whole walk - countryside, woodland, rivers, navigation's, historic houses and street walking. You start from Cockfosters and head eastwards through Trent Park and Enfield Chase to Hilly Fields Park and Forty Hall. Here you follow Turkey Brook and cross the historic New River before walking through Enfield Wash to the

River Lee Navigation. A short walk from here brings you to Enfield Lock Railway Station and buses. A picturesque walk along near the northern boundary of the Borough of Enfield. The route is well signed with the distinctive London Loop logo.

WALKING INSTRUCTIONS - Turn right out of Cockfosters Underground Station and right again onto the path on the immediate left of car park. Follow the tarmaced path with a cemetery on your left to an oak tree and open field. Turn left along its lefthand side along a wide path, over a footbridge and onto woodland. Keep along its lefthand side before turning left into an open field. Keep to the righthand side with Church Wood on your right and gain the entrance drive into Trent Country Park. Cross the road and follow the road on the left of an obelisk on whose base are the words - *"These gardens were begun in the Year 1706 and at several times inlarged altered and Adorned to this year 1740." Note the spelling!*

On you right is the main car park. Keep ahead and reach the Park Cafe on your left. Keep straight ahead into woodland and immediately pass Section 17 Notice Board of the London Loop on your right. The path through Oak Wood curves right to the wood's end. Continue ahead with the hedge on your left to the next wood. Don't enter, but turn left and curve right on the path with the first lake on your right, as you walk along a driveway. Reaching a junction of paths/tracks with the start of the second and larger lake on your right, turn left and ascend through woodland. Where the path/drive's fork, keep to the lefthand one, still in woodland. A little later keep left again and to your right is the entrance to Camlet Moat - English Heritage - *one of the best examples of a moated site, occupied between 1150-1500 AD.* Follow the path left and as you near Hadley Road, turn right to it.

Turn left beside the road and you can see another obelisk just outside the trees on your left. In a few yards reach a small lay-by and turn right at a kissing gate and follow the path downhill past Ash Wood on your left, to the bottom. Follow the path sharp right with a fence on your right and hedge on your left. You basically keep to the valley floor for the next 1 1/4 miles (25 mins.). In 1/2 mile reach a stile and cross a footbridge and turn right to walk along the righthand side of the field, beside Salmon's Brook. Cross two more stiles before reaching the field corner - all part of Enfield Chase - and as footpath signed bear left and ascend the righthand side of the field. Near the top turn right at a kissing gate into woodland - "Planted in 1991 in memory of Councillor Roger Brooke." Follow the path to a stile and along close to the road - The Ridgeway (A1005), before reaching it. To your right - southwards - you have views to central London with The Gherkin and Alexandra Palace being prominent.

Turn right along the road and pass The Chace Hotel on the right. Soon after turn left and descend the drive to Rectory Farm. Follow the farm track (concrete) - bridleway - right past a "No Galloping" sign and ascend past The Red House on the right. Cross the railway line and reach a path junction. Turn right onto another track and follow it uphill to houses and a tarmaced road - Strayfield Lane. Keep ahead and near the end of the road - Fallow Buck Inn just ahead, turn right onto a tarmaced path into Hilly Fields Park. Follow the path as it gently descends to Turkey Brook. Cross a footbridge and turn left along a tarmaced path with the brook on your left. At the next footbridge bear right uphill on the tarmaced path and at the top turn left and gradually descend the tarmaced path to a London Loop Section 17 history board, a gate and road with the Rose & Crown Inn opposite.

Cross the road and keep straight ahead on the righthand side of the inn. For the next mile keep the brook on your left. First reach a path junction, with the Old Course of the New River on your right, and keep straight ahead. 1/4 mile later reach another stile and keep right to continue by the brook on your left as you walk along a wide path in Forty Hall Park. In 1/2 mile pass a lake on your right and a small one, which in summer if covered with yellow lilies. Continue to the Forty Hill road and turn right and left to gain it, opposite Forty Hall Primary School. Turn left then right to continue on a tarmaced path and soon cross the New River. Keep straight ahead to the A10 road. Cross via the footbridge and turn left and right to continue on a tarmaced path with Enfield cemetery on your right. At the end cross the footbridge over the railway line, near Turkey Street Station. Just after reach Winnington Road, Turn left along it to Turkey Street; the station is just to your left.

Turn right along Turkey Street and pass The Turkey Inn and soon reach the A1010 road (Hertford Road) at Enfield Wash. Cross and turn right past Tommy's Bar and left along the first road on your left, St. Stephen's Road. At the end turn right and left onto a footpath and keep Turkey Brook on your left and soon have Albany Park on your right. Keep straight ahead and cross the footbridge over the railway line to Enfield Lock Station (to your left). Just after turn left then right to continue with the brook now on your right. Later keep right and cross the road bridge over Mollison Avenue (A1055). Keep ahead to the road opposite Enfield Lock on the River Lee Navigation.

Here you leave the London Loop and turn left along the navigation to being

THE LONDON LOOP - 10 MILES
- *Map Two* - FORTY HALL
TO ENFIELD LOCK

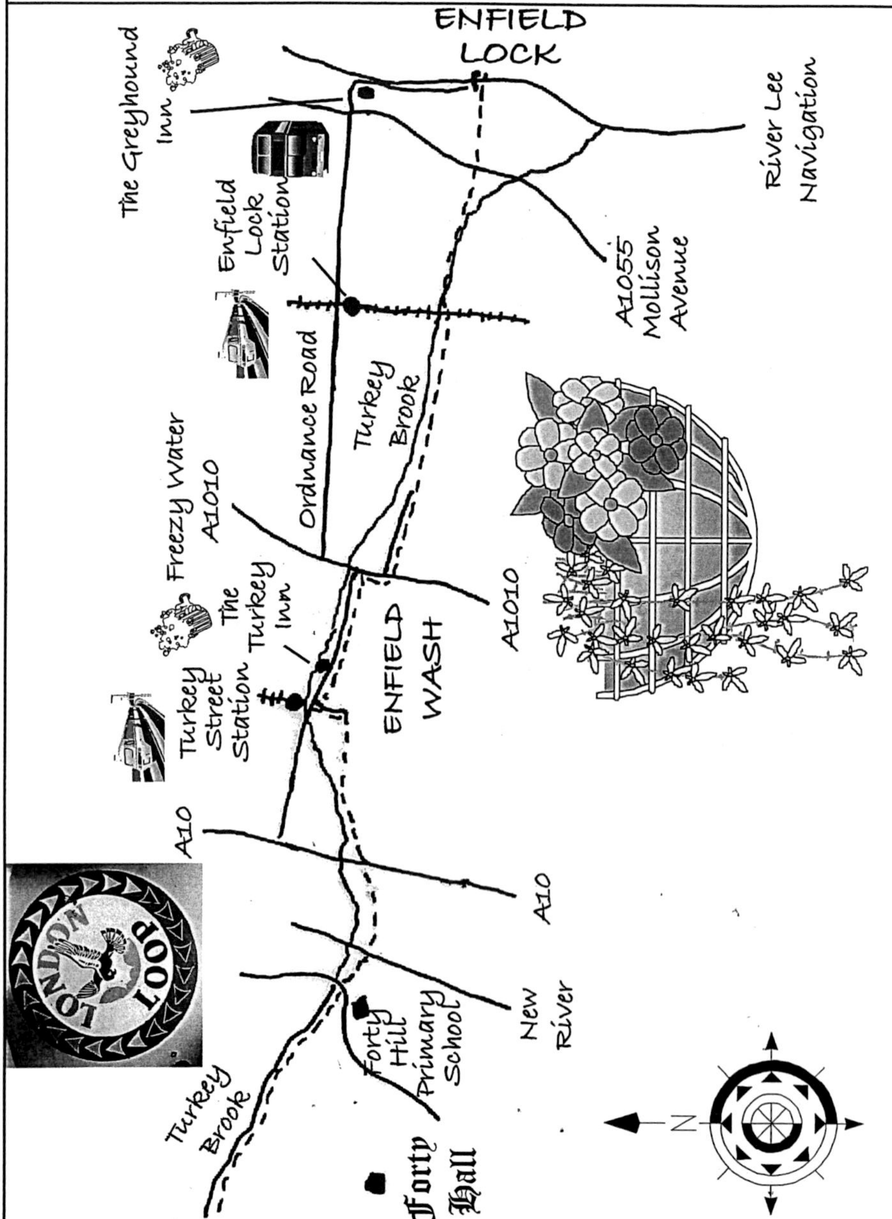

level with the Greyhound Inn. Turn left and reach Mollison Avenue. Cross and keep ahead along Ordnance Road to bus stop and Enfield Lock Station.

THE LONDON LOOP - a 150 circular walk around the outskirts of London. The word loop is derived from the first letters of - **L**ondon **O**uter **O**rbital **P**ath. The whole route is broken down into 24 sections as it passes through 14 London Borough's. It is a delightful and surprising walk, which can be done in stages, as each section ends beside a bus or train/ underground station.

CAMLET MOAT - Locally excavated in the 1850's by Emma Francis Shuttleworth of Trent Park. First they uncovered part of a red-tiled roof. Excavating deeper they uncovered a dungeon with a wall chain and glazed tiles with knight on horseback.

ENFIELD CHASE - Once the Royal hunting area of Kings and Queens, it is now one of the largest green spaces in London with several farms.

RIVER LEE NAVIGATION - PICKETT'S LOCK TO ENFIELD LOCK - 5 MILES

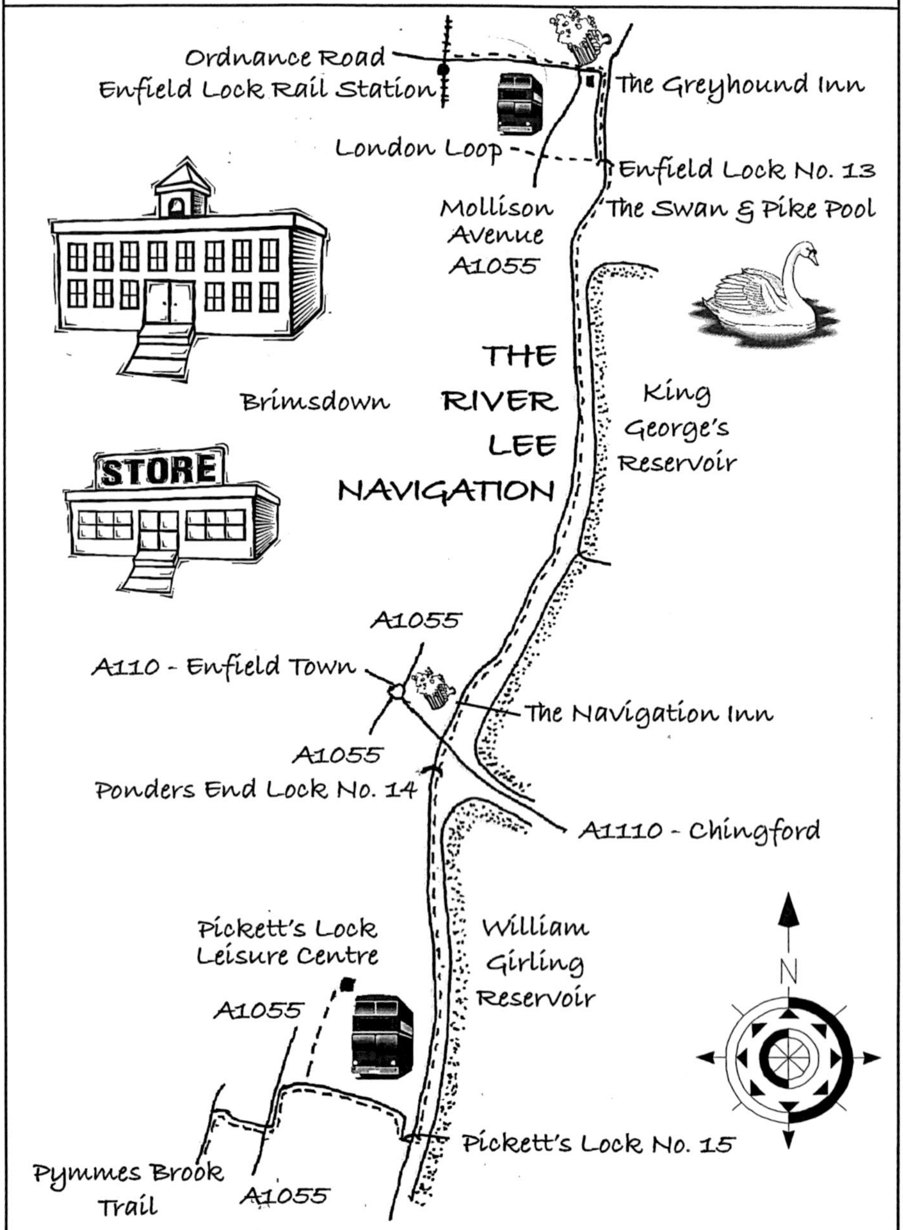

RIVER LEE NAVIGATION - PICKETT'S LOCK TO ENFIELD LOCK - 5 MILES - allow 3 hours

Basic route - Pickett's Lock Leisure Centre - Pickett's Lock - River Lee Navigation - Ponders End Lock - Swan & Pike Pool - Enfield Lock - Enfield Lock Station.

Map - O. S. 1:25,000 Explorer Series No. 173 - London North.

Start - Pickett's Lock Leisure Centre, reached via bus No. W8.
End - Enfield Lock Rail Station or Bus No. 121.

Inns - The Greyhound Inn, Enfield Lock.

Cafe - Ordnance Road, Enfield Lock.

ABOUT THE WALK - The River Lee Navigation is an outstanding waterway along eastern side of the Borough of Enfield. It is a delightful one way walk in its own right, watching the swans and ducks, as narrowboats glide by. Alternatively you can add it onto the Pymmes Brook Trail (Pickett's Lock) or London Loop walks (Enfield Lock), making two walks of 15 miles. As I live on the Enfield side of Waltham Cross, I always add this onto my walks, otherwise I don't feel as though I have had a full day out!

WALKING INSTRUCTIONS - Starting from Pickett's Lock Leisure Centre, walk southwards along the road past the car park on the right and athletics stadium on the left. Keep straight ahead to the junction with Pickett's Lock Lane. Turn left and follow this road and where it curves right to a car park, turn left past Burdens and cross the navigation to Pickett's Lock No. 15. To your right the navigation heads southwards towards Limehouse basin and the River Thames, with some of London's skyline visible. There are picnic tables beside the lock.

Turn left and follow the defined path along the righthand side of the navigation - you keep to this side all the way to Enfield Lock more than 3 miles away. In one mile reach Ponders End Lock No. 14 and pass under the A110 road. Just ahead and on the otherside of the navigation is The Navigation Inn (Harvester). Keep beside the navigation on your left and in more than two miles (45 mins) reach the Swan and Pike Pool on the right, with a London Loop Information Board. Continue ahead across a footbridge and onto the road just before Enfield Lock No. 13. Go left across the bridge and then right to continue on the towpath with the navigation now on your right. Before the next road bridge, a little over 1/4 mile from the lock, leave the navigation and join the road past The Greyhound Inn (dates from 1867), to traffic lights and Mollison Avenue (A1055). Go straight across and walk along Ordnance Road to either the bus stop or Enfield Lock Rail Station.

RIVER LEE NAVIGATION - Some brief history notes -

Length - Limehouse Basin, Bow to Hertford - 27 3/4 miles. 19 locks.

The River Lee has been, since Roman times, an important trade route to London. An Act of 1571 for an artificial cut was made to help speed up the traffic. At the same time a pound at Waltham Abbey with lock gates - a similar principal to today - was made and is one of the earliest in the country. During the 18th and 19th. century the navigation was improved, these included in 1769 the Waltham, Edmonton and Hackney Cuts (avoiding the River Lee) and pound locks was opened. In 1911 The Lee Conservancy bought the River Stort Navigation and improved it together with the River Lee. By 1930, 130 ton boats could reach Enfield and 100 ton to Ware and Hertford. During the rest of the 20th. century many improvements were made including mechanised locks. Whilst many of the locks vary in size the majority are - 85 ft long by 16 ft wide and between 5 and 7 feet deep. Upto Enfield Lock they are double locks and beyond to Hertford, single locks. The river can be either spelt Lee or Lea. The navigation forms part of a 50 mile Lea Valley walk from Limehouse Basin to Luton.

Pickett's Lock, looking north.

THE LEE VALLEY REGIONAL PARK - The first regional park in Britain, now covering 10,000 acres, along 26 miles of the River Lee (Lea). There are many picnic areas, car parks along its length, with excellent bus and rail links.

ROYAL SMALL ARMS FACTORY - Was where the famous Lee & Enfield Rifles were made. The site is now the Island Housing Estate. At onetime there was a ferry across the River Lee Navigation, opposite the Greyhound Inn, to take workers into the factory complex.

Enfield Lock, looking north.

ENFIELD TOWN & FORTY HILL HISTORICAL WALK - 4 MILES

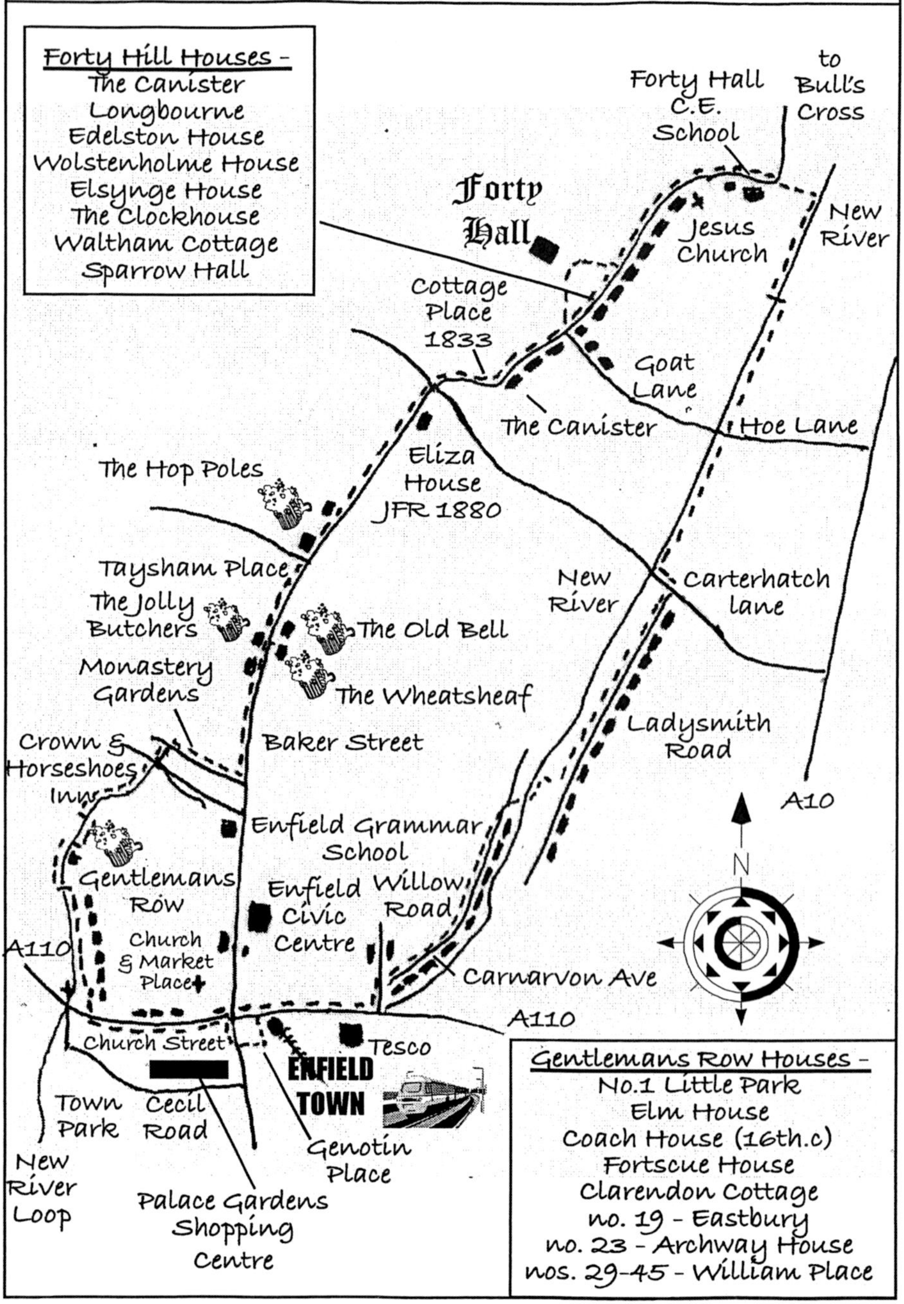

ENFIELD TOWN & FORTY HILL HISTORICAL WALK 1 4 MILES - allow 2 or more hours.

Basic route - Enfield Town Station - Genotin Place - Church Street - Gentleman's Row - New River Loop - Monastery Gardens - Baker Street - Forty Hill - New River - Enfield Town Station.

Map - O.S. 1:25,000 Explorer Series No. 173 - London North.

Start and end - Enfield Town Station.
Several buses stop here, including - 121, 191, 231, 307, 313, and 317.

Inns - Numerous on the walk first mile to Forty Hill - in walking order - The Stag, Crown & Horseshoes Inn, The Jolly Butchers, The Wheatsheaf, The Old Bell, The Hop Poles. The Goose at the George Inn, in Church Street, Enfield, near the start.

Cafe - Several along Church Street in Enfield.

ABOUT THE WALK - A walk that encompasses all the historical buildings in Enfield Town and Forty Hill - there are an amazing number. You return along quiet paths beside the New River back to Enfield. I have started the walk from Enfield Town station, on purpose, as almost next door is the first historical building. You can get here by train or by the many different buses. Set off an explore the history and see for yourself the wealth of exceptional buildings, on your doorstep!

WALKING INSTRUCTIONS - Turn left out of the station and immediately left along the road - Genotin Road - and cross to the righthand side. After 75 yards turn left along Genotin Place, a fine row of of early 19th. century buildings, to the next road - London Road - with the Palace Gardens Shopping Centre opposite. Turn right to the cross roads. Before turning left along Church

Genotin Place.

Street, it is worth while walking straight ahead, along Silver Street, towards Enfield Civic Centre, to see some historic buildings including the White Lodge and opposite is the monument to the WW2 Arctic Campaign Convoys.

St. Andrews Vicarage - dates back to the 15th. century.

White Lodge - Early 18th century white painted weather board building. In the 19th. century was the home of Joseph Whitaker - 1820 - 1895, the founder and publisher of Whitaker's Almanacs.

Enfield Civic Centre - The tower block built in the 1970's and originally contained the individual borough's of Enfield, Southgate and Edmonton.

Return to the cross roads and turn right along Church Street. On the left is the granite tri-corn water fountain (1884/5) and The Goose at the George Inn. Rebuilt in 1895 and originally known as The George. An inn has stood on this site since 1548. On the right is the building dated 1897, was once Enfield's tallest building. On the right is The Old Vestry.

A few yards later on your right is the Market Place and church; both worth a visit.

The present Market Place dates from 1632, but the Market dates from 1616. The water pump remains but the stocks and whipping post have long gone. The octagonal wooden Market House was built in 1904, to commemorate the Coronation of King Edward 7th. The Kings Head was built in 1899 and an inn has stood here since 1548.

St. Andrews Church - The tower and nave are 14th. century. The north aisle was built a century later and the south aisle was rebuilt in 1826. On the left of the chancel is the large and impressive 17th. century marble monument to Sir Nicholas Rainton, the builder of Forty Hall, and his wife, Lady Rebecca.

Next is the National Westminster Bank and the historic plaque of the first *"Hole in the Wall."*

Continue to the end of Church Street and turn right into Little Park Gardens and cross the road to the right of The Stag Inn, to the left is Trinity Church, to walk along Gentlemen's Row - mostly Grade I I listed buildings - an "Outstanding Conservation Area."

Trinity Church - built in 1889 by Wesleyan Methodist's; there are several stones in the front, stating when they were placed in 1889 and by whom.

17th. century marble monument to Sir Nicholas Rainton in St. Andrews Church.

No. 1 Gentleman's Row.

Gentleman's Row in walking order -

No 1 - Registry Office & Trading Standards Office - formerly Little Park and an exceptional fine Georgian building. In 1888 was sold to the Enfield Local Board of Health and is today the Registry Office. The central three storey block is topped by a pediment. In the centre the first floor window has a pediment and balustrade.

Next door, No. 5, is the new Little Park. Mostly Edwardian but some parts are much earlier. The south extension, built in 1926, is known as the Tudor Room, for here are parts of Enfield Palace (c1550) and includes panelling, ceiling and fireplace.

Elm House - 18th. century red bricked. It has been a girls and boys school and a Convalescent Home for soldiers.

Fortescue Lodge, No. 11 - dates from the 17th. century with a 19th. century white front.

Coach House - built in the 16th. century as a barn; it later became the coach house for Fortescue Hall which was demolished in 1813.

No. 17 - Clarendon Cottage - Parts date back to the 16th century. A plaque to Charles Lamb is on the side and he stayed here in 1825 and 1827. He lived later in Edmonton - see the Edmonton walk - pages 46 to 57 - for his cottage and grave.

Clarendon Cottage.

No. 19 - Eastbury - The red bricked front is 18th. century, which hides a 17th. century timber frame structure.

No. 21 - Red brick with large doorway.

No. 23 - Archway House - Built about 1750 and for a while, in the late 19th. century, was Archway Tavern, named after its impressive arch doorway. The central bay is topped by a large pediment.

Nos. 29-45 - William Place - built in 1871.

At the end bear left across the bridge over the New River Loop into River View and another row of delightful houses, although more recent. Turn right to the Crown and Horseshoes Inn.

Crown & Horseshoes Inn - Charles Lamb was a frequent visitor here, as he lived for a while in Gentlemen's Row. The inn is associated with the brutal murder of Danby.

The Crown & Horseshoes Inn and New River Loop.

Cross the footbridge (1841) and follow the path left to the next footbridge. Cross and turn right along the path with the river on your right. Follow the path to a New River History board and onto the road - Parsonage Lane. Go straight across into Monastery Gardens and follow the road round to your right to the main road - Baker Street.

Monastery Gardens was formerly Parsonage Lane names after a Parsonage that stood here. This was demolished to make way for the housing.

Turn left and pass several inns - ***The Jolly Butchers*** - recorded in 1841 and rebuilt in 1907. ***The Wheatsheaf*** - rebuilt early in the 20th. century - and ***the Old Bell*** - the original building had a date stone of 1502, and was rebuilt in the late 19th. century.

Also pass ***No. 174 Baker Street***, another red bricked building dating from the early 18th. century. Red tiled gabled roof and dormer windows. Over the doorway is a circular window.

Then pass Taysham Place, on the left, before the road junction and The Hop Poles Inn opposite.

Hop Poles Inn - Originally, in 1838, the inn was two cottages. It has since been rebuilt twice and current building dates from 1909. The name Hop Poles refers to the stilts used to pick the hops.

Continue straight ahead, still on Baker Street. As you approach Carterhatch Road on the right is Eliza House with date plaque - 1880. On the left, the white painted house no. 470 has a blue plaque to - *"Capt. Frederick Marryat - 1792 - 1848 - Novelist, was educated at 'Holmwood' on this site."*

Go straight across and pass ornate gates on the left then Cottage Place, 1833 - yellow brick with red brick dressings. Keep straight ahead along Forty Hill and pass in walking order several Grade I I listed buildings -

The Canister, 29 Forty Hill - 18th. century and said to resemble a tea canister; hence its name. It is really a most pleasant building to the eye, being a Georgian Villa with four large arches.

Forty Hill House - Georgian building; built in the late 18th. century and has a 19th. century Doric porch.

Longbourn - Long two storey building built in three stages. The central five bays was built about 1720. The northern extension in about 1800 and the southern extension and porch is mid Victorian.

The past Edelston House and Wolstenholme House. Next is -

Elsynge House - red brick 18th. century (mid to late) house with delightful windows - the ground floor are Venetian styled with the first floor semicircular.

No. 78 - The Hermitage - Large house of six bays, two storey's high. and built in 1704. The rear is earlier dates from the 1620's.

Forty Hall - built for Sir Nicholas Rainton, a Lord Mayor of London, between 1629 and 1636. Bought by the Enfield Council in the 1950's and now houses a museum, cafe and function suite. Free entrance with the grounds used for a variety of events. *See separate walk for more details.*

Goat Lane - on the righthand corner the house was formerly the Goat Inn. The inn was first mentioned in 1721 and became a private residence in 1929. A new Goat Inn was built opposite Cottage Place, further down Forty Hill, in 1929, and is now "Chimneys House." While on the other corner is the red bricked Worcester Lodge built in 1704.

The Clockhouse - Large 19th. century building converted to flats.

Waltham Cottage - 18th. century.

Sparrow Hall - 18th. century and in the 19th. century was the vicarage for Jesus Church. This is now next door.

Continue downhill and pass ***Jesus Church*** - built in 1835 by a Tottenham builder, Thomas Ashwell - and then ***Forty Hill C. E. School*** - dates from 1851 - on the right. Just after and before the traffic lights and Maidens Bridge, turn right on the signed footpath, which is also part of the London Loop.

There are more historical buildings of Enfield ahead along the road, but it is road walking. These include houses at Bulls Cross, and the Pied Bull Inn and Myddleton House.

In a short distance reach the piped New River and turn right through a kissing and ascend to the New River. Follow the path with the river on your left to a footbridge. Cross and continue on the path along the lefthand side of the river to kissing gates and Hoe Lane.

Go straight across and continue with the river on your right to the next road - Carterhatch Lane and kissing gate. Turn left and 100 yards later right along Ladysmith Road. Keep straight ahead along the road and past a road barrier. Continue to immediately before house no. 172 and turn right into Lambourne Gardens. At the end turn left on the path and rejoin, briefly, the New River. Cross the footbridge and follow the path to the first road - Carnarvon Avenue.

Turn left and follow this road. Where it divides, keep left along Apple Grove to continue to a road circle. Beyond it is a path that leads to Willow Road - most of the houses here date from the 1930's. Turn left to the main road - Southbury Road, with Tesco opposite. Turn right to join a piece of the New River Loop on your right. Here are several bus stops and a little further on your left is Enfield Town Station.

Elm House, Gentleman's Row.

PONDERS END, RIVER LEE, BRIMSDOWN & DURANTS PARK - 6 MILES

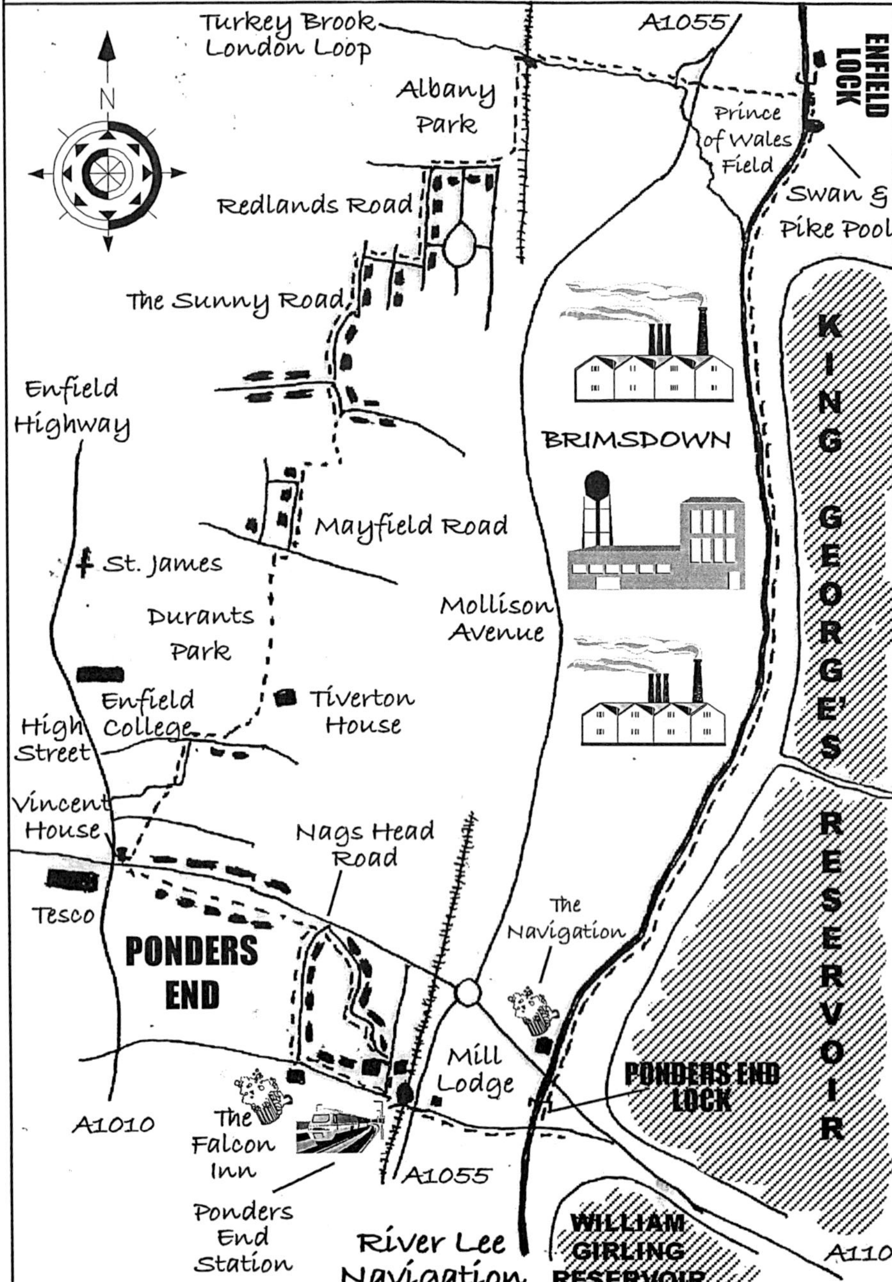

PONDERS END, RIVER LEE NAVIGATION, BRIMSDOWN & DURANTS PARK - 6 MILES - allow 2 1/2 hours.

Basic route - Ponders End, High Street - Scotland Green Road - The Falcon Inn - Ponders End Station - Ponders End Lock, No. 14 - River Lee Navigation - Enfield Lock, No. 13 - Prince of Wales Field - London Loop - Albany Park - The Brightside - The Sunny Road - Brimsdown Bowls Club - Durants Park - Durants Road - Nags Head Road - Ponders End, High Street.

Map - O.S. 1:25,000 Explorer Series No. 173 - London North.

Start/end - Ponders End, High Street at the junction of Southbury Road/Nags Head Road (A110 & A1010 roads). Bus Nos. 279, 191, 349 & 491.

- alternative start/end - Ponders End Station, actually on the route, or Southbury Station. If the later simply turn right out of the station and descend Southbury Road, past Tesco's to the cross roads; the walk starts across the road (High Street), on the right.

Inns - The Falcon Inn near Ponders End Station. Less than 1/4 mile off the route at Enfield Lock is The Greyhound Inn. Others on Ponders End, High Street, just off the route at the end!

ABOUT THE WALK - The walk is a complete mixed bag of scenery. First you walk along *"Garage Alley"*, as I call it, before passing tower blocks to Ponders End Station. After crossing the rail footbridge you pass a historic mill before gaining the tranquil River Lee Navigation. Now in countryside with sheep grazing and waterfowl on the navigation, you pass the industrial heartland of the borough, at Brimsdown, on the left. At Enfield Lock close to where the world renowned Lee & Enfield rifles were made, you join briefly the London Loop. After 1/2 mile you leave it to walk through Albany Park, before following paths and pavements to Durants Park. Just after you are back at Ponders End, High Street, surprised at what the area has to offer.

WALKING INSTRUCTIONS - Starting from the cross roads at Ponders End High Street - Southbury Road/Nags Head Road and High Street. Cross to the righthand side of Nags Head Road, with Vincent House on the left corner. Just ahead is a footpath sign. Basically keep straight ahead along the tarmaced drive and pass numerous garages, as you walk along "Garage Alley". Follow it for nearly 1/2 mile to Scotland Green Road, with Curzon Avenue opposite. To your left is the Nags Head Road and round the corner is the Catholic church - Mary, Mother of God. If you do not want The Falcon Inn, cross the road into Curzon Avenue and follow it right and left to the tower block, Cormorant and right to South Street passing another tower block on the left, Kestrel. Turn left along South Street, past shops on the left to Ponders End Station.

If wanting to visit the inn, turn right along Scotland Green Road and follow it to South Street, with The Falcon Inn opposite. Turn left to Ponders End Station.

At the station walk across the footbridge and over the A1055 road to Wharf Road. Here on the left can be seen the 18th century Mill Lodge and Ponders End Mill beyond. Keep ahead along the road, over the River Lee and almost immediately after the River Lee Navigation. On it righthand side turn left and gain the towpath and Ponders End Lock, No. 14 - a double lock. Head northwards along the towpath, passing a plaque about Otters, who now inhabit the area - a sign of a healthy river. Follow the towpath for more than two miles to Enfield Lock, No. 13. In the final stages you pass the Swan & Pike Pool and car park on the right.

Ponders End Lock, No. 14.

Enfield Lock No. 13.

Infront of the lock on the road bridge, turn left, now on the London Loop, and follow the footpath, as signed, to pass the Prince of Wales Field on the left and Primary School on the right. Follow the path to a footbridge over the A1055 road (Mollison Avenue). Keep straight ahead with Turkey Brook on your left. Pass houses on your right. Cross a road - Bilton Way - and soon after turn left over a footbridge over the brook, and then right over a footbridge over the railway line to Albany Park. Immediately turn left, leaving the London Loop, and follow the tarmaced path by the metal fence on the left. Alternatively, you can walk through the "hills" and silver birch trees, just to the right. Both paths lead to the otherside of the park and Bell Lane.

Turn right and take the third road on your left - Redlands Road. In 1/4 mile (5 mins), take the first road on your right, The Brightside. Follow it across a road, past houses to The Sunny Road. Turn left and follow it, soon following it right and left to reach Carterhatch Road. Keep straight ahead along this road to where it turns left. Here, keep ahead, as path signed. Follow the tarmaced path passed houses and no. 189, and immediately after house no. 85, turn right, still on the tarmaced path. On your left is a football field. Follow the path round to your left to Mayfield Road, with the Brimsdown Bowling Club, founded in 1993, on your left. Keep ahead along Mayfield Road to the next road - Green Street - with shops on your left.

Cross to your right and walk along the tarmaced path into Durants Park. Follow the tarmaced path, with St. James church cemetery to your right. Follow the path round to the right, with Enfield College at the end of the park, on the right. Pass Tiverton House tower block on the left and reach a road - The Ridge. Turn right and then left along Cowland Avenue - No Through Road. Follow it round to the right and here on the left is the signed footpath - between houses no. 54 & 56. Follow the path to Durants Road. Go straight across and continue on the tarmaced path to the Nags Head Road; opposite is your starting out path. On your right is Vincent House (Enfield's Citizen's Advice Bureau) and Ponders End High Street. To the left along the High Street,are inns and the bus stop.

Mill House Lodge.

PONDERS END MILL - G. R. Wright & Sons Ltd., - The only working flour mill on the River Lea, whose origins go back some 900 years. Now part of a conservation area with several listed buildings. George Reynolds Wright in 1867, went into partnership with the then owner, James Dilly Young. Upon his death, Wright carried on assisted by his sons. No longer water powered, it is now operated by electricity. The original 18th. century mill building remains, as does the red bricked Mill House and lodge, which can be seen from Wharf Road; note the windows. The business is arguably the oldest still running, in Enfield, and certainly one with the longest history!

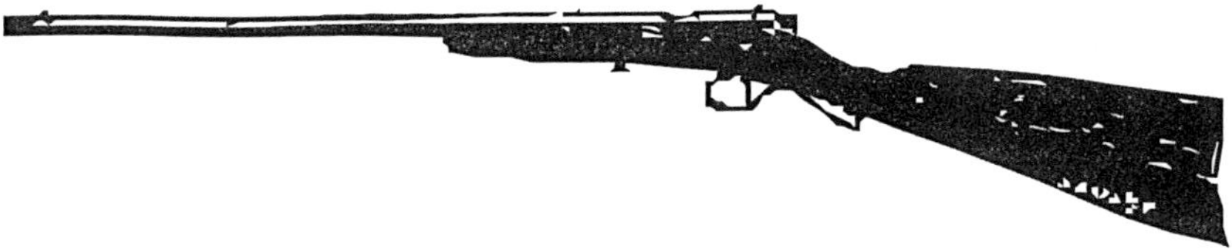

LEE AND ENFIELD RIFLES - The Royal Small Arms Factory was built here, at Enfield Lock in 1812 and described then, as being, "remote and picturesque." The site grew and became almost self contained with its own Police force, church, school, canteen and an inn - originally known as the Swan and Pike - but lately as The Rifles. Here were made the famous Lee-Enfield and the Martini-Henry Rifles, which the British Troops used in the Boer War and both WW1 and WW2. The factory closed down in 1987 and is today an impressive housing estate, with canal arm. Just a little further along the Lee Navigation from Enfield Lock can be seen on the right, Government Row, a row of delightful terrace houses, built as workers accommodation; a fine example of Industrial buildings. A few more paces and on the left is The Greyhound Inn. A punt ferry existed here to ferry workers across the Lee Navigation to the factory.

Canal mooring - South Island Marina, near Ponders End Lock.

GO FOR IT!

THE ENFIELD CIRCULAR CHALLENGE WALK - 25 MILES - allow 9 hours.

Basic route - Cockfosters - Pymmes Brook Trail to Pickett's Lock - River Lee Navigation - Enfield Lock - London Loop back to Cockfosters.

Map - O.S. 1:25,000 Explorer Series No. 173 - London North.

ABOUT THE WALK - Not quite a "beating of the bounds", but a circular walk around Enfield, which you can start and end anywhere on the route. You can do the London Loop section first, then the River Lee and back along the Pymmes Brook Trail. For walking instructions see the last three walks in this book.

For those who successfully complete the walk either in a day or in stages, a special signed certificate is available from me! Just send me your details and when you did the walk for the certificate.

Happy walking!

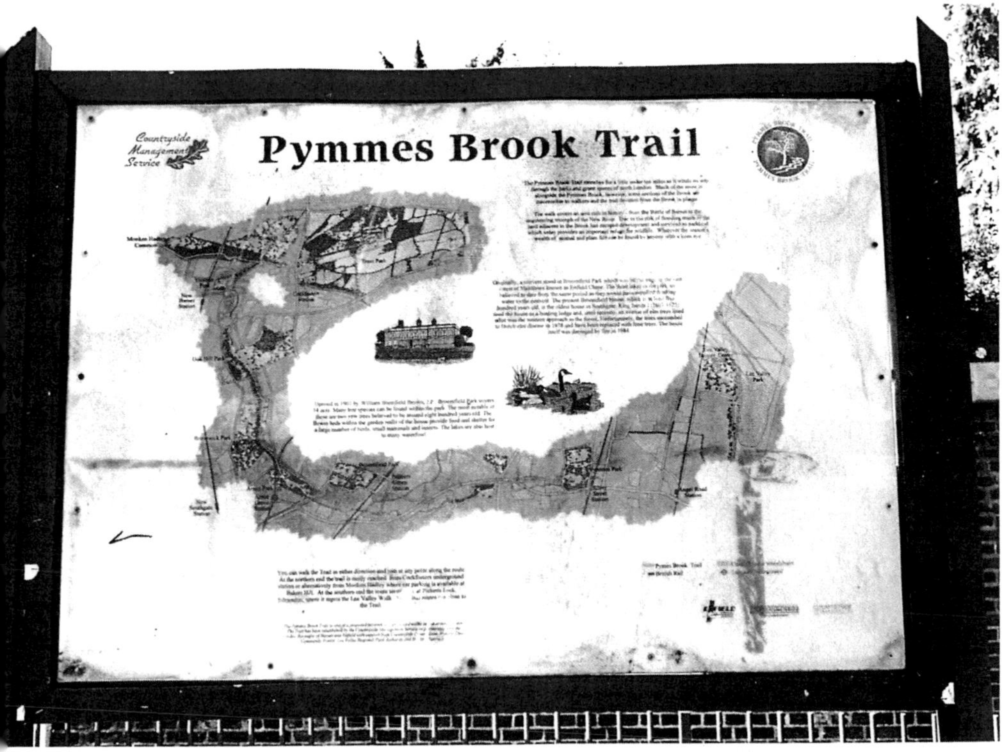

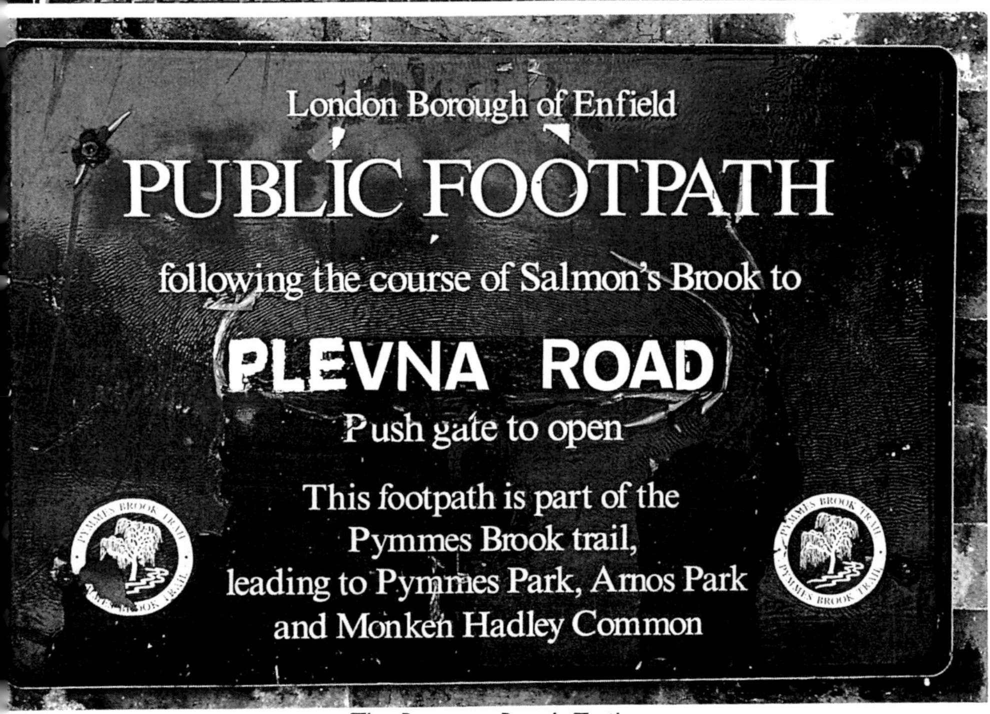

The Pymmes Brook Trail.

London Loop logo.

Looking south from Pickett's Lock.

WALK RECORD CHART

Date Walked -

Enfield Town park & New River Loop - 2 miles ....

Enfield Parks and New River - 7 miles ....

The New River in Enfield - 8 miles ....

Around Trent Country Park - 4 miles ....

Forty Hall, Whitewebbs Park and Hilly Fields Park - 4 1/2 miles ....

Southgate - Grovelands Park - 2 miles ....

Walking the streets of Edmonton - 5 miles ....

The Pymmes Brook Trail - 10 miles ....

The London Loop, in Enfield - 10 miles ....

The River Lee Navigation - Pickett's Lock to Enfield Lock - 5 miles ....

Enfield Town & Forty Hill Historical Walk - 4 miles ....

Ponders End, River Lee, Brimsdown & Durants Park - 6 miles ....

The Enfield Circular Challenge Walk - 25 miles ....

THE JOHN MERRILL SHORT WALK BADGE

Complete FOUR walks in this book and get the above special embroidered badge and signed certificate. Badges are Black cloth with lettering and hiker embroidered in four colours.

BADGE ORDER FORM

Date of Enfield walks completed...

NAME ....

ADDRESS ....

....

Price: £6.00 each including postage, packing, VAT and signed completion certificate. Amount enclosed (Payable to The John Merrill Foundation).

From: The John Merrill Foundation,
32, Holmesdale, Waltham Cross,
Hertsfordshire, EN8 8QY
Fax/Tel - 01992 - 762776
E-mail - john@thejohnmerrillwalkguides.co.uk

HAPPY WALKING T SHIRT - £10 inc. P&P

********** YOU MAY PHOTOCOPY THIS FORM ***********

THE LONDON BOROUGHS WALKS SERIES

Each book explores all the walks within the boundaries of the borough, including sections of the recreational paths - The Capital Ring and London Loop. Also all waymarked paths in each borough and along any canal or navigation. Paths/ routes linking parks together are also written about. Plus details of shorter walks in Open Spaces and Nature Reserves. Each book attempts to cover all the walks in each borough, together with considerable local history, adding interest and purpose to each walk. Details of how to get to a walks' start by bus, underground and train is included, together with details of what Ordnance Survey map is needed, plus inns and cafe's along the way. Combined, all you need to explore a given area of London. London has much to offer the walker and explorer and it is hope these walks will prove an eye-opener to the historic countryside on your doorstep.
....*Happy walking!*

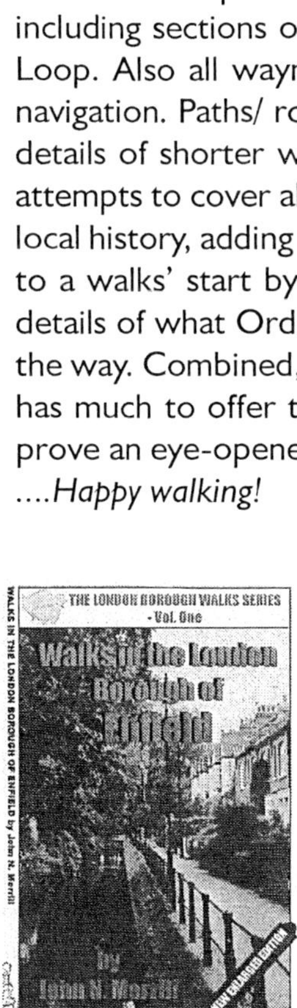

Vol. One - WALKS IN THE LONDON BOROUGH OF ENFIELD

The London Borough of Enfield, is London's most northern borough, with some 40 miles of footpaths. Passing through the area are the signed paths of the London Loop, River Lee Navigation, Pymmes Brook Trail and the New River. They provide rewarding countryside walking, but the borough has much more to offer. With some delightful town parks and country parks. Added to this are some fascinating buildings, in Enfield and Edmonton, and a rich history, providing enjoyable walks in both town and countryside.

Here are twleve walks and a 25 miles challenge walk, which explore the Borough fully; whether you are a local or not, the walks will come as a pleasant surprise in the surrounding suburbia.

New Enlarged Edition.

A5 wire bound. 104 pages. 16 maps. 43 photographs. £9.95

ISBN 978-0-955651 1-2-0

Vol. Two - WALKS IN THE LONDON BOROUGH OF BARNET

Includes historical walks in Barnet and around the Battle of Barnet area. The Dollis Valley Green Walk, the Pymmes Brook Trail, The London Loop and Capital Ring sections in the borough. Plus walks around Totteridge and Mill Hill, Edgware and many of the parks, including Sunnyhill, Brunswick Park, Oak Hill Park and Stoneyfields Park. 15 walks plus suggestions for other short walks. Combined they encompass the whole of the borough.

A5. 124 Pages. 18 maps. 43 photographs. Wire Bound.
£9.95
ISBN 978-0-9556511-4-4

Vol. Three - WALKS IN THE LONDON BOROUGH OF HARINGEY

12 walks, includes historical walks inTottenham High Road, Park walks, the New River, Capital Ring and River Lee Navigation - Tottenham Marshes - the scene of the Tottenham Outrage. Other walks explore the parks of Tottenham, Muswell Hill, Crouch End, Hornsey and to some of the stunning hidden places - parks and woods - of the borough. Alexandra Palace and Park, has its own walk around this amazing place. One 12 mile walk totally encircles the borough.

96 pages. 71photographs. 11 maps.
A5. Wire bound. £9.95.
ISBN 978-0-9556511-8-2

Vol. Four - WALKS IN THE LONDON BOROUGH OF WALTHAM FOREST

Includes historical walks in Chingford, Leyton and Walthamstow, the River Lee Navigation and Epping Forest. A 24 mile boundary walk, a walk around Walthamstow Village, and walks in conservation areas and parks. 15 walks altogether.

120 pages. 18 maps. 65 photographs. A5. Wire bound.

OTHER NORTH LONDON WALK BOOKS
by JOHN N. MERRILL

SHORT CIRCULAR WALKS ON THE RIVER LEE NAVIGATION - Northern Volume - Ponder's End - Hertford. 64 pages, 23 photographs, 10 detailed maps and walks. History notes.
- ISBN 1-903627-68-0 @ £8.50

WALKING THE RIVER LEE NAVIGATION - VOL 1 & 2.

SHORT CIRCULAR WALKS ON THE NEW RIVER & SOUTH EAST HERTFORDSHIRE
11 walks - 5 to 10 miles long between Waltham Cross and Hertford; many on the New River. New revised and enlarged edition 80 pages, 24 photographs , 13 detailed maps. History notes.
ISBN 1-903627-69-9 @ £8.95

SHORT CIRCULAR WALKS IN EPPING FOREST
10 circular walks 6 to 18 miles long. Combined they explore the whole forest and its surrounding area. 68 pages. 12 maps. 30 photographs. History notes.
ISBN 1-903627-72-9 @ £8.50

LONG CIRCULAR WALKS IN EASTERN HERTFORDSHIRE
9 walks - 15 to 20 miles long. Beautiful unspoilt walking in rolling countryside full of historical interest. £10.95
ISBN 978-0-9553691-7-9

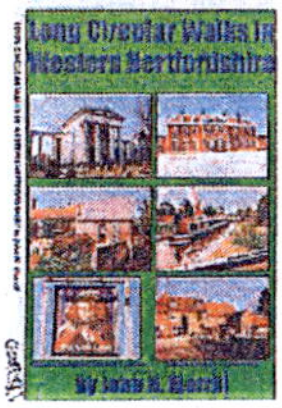

LONG CIRCULAR WALKS IN WESTERN HERTFORDSHIRE -
9 long walks - 15 to 20 miles.. 112 pages. Wire bound. 55 photographs. 20detailed maps. £10.95
ISBN 978-0-955651113

SHORT CIRCULAR WALKS AROUND HERTFORD.
3 historical Town walks and four country walks.
ISBN 978-0-955651 1-7-5 £9.95

NEW - SHORT CIRCULAR WALKS AROUND BISHOP' STORTFORD

SHORT CIRCULAR WALKS ON THE RIVER STORT NAVIGATION
8 circular walks; 1 End to End walk. Full history and photographic study of this peaceful waterway. 92 pages. 68 photographhs. 12 maps. ISBN 1-903627- 73-7 £11.95

SHORT CIRCULAR WALKS ON THE RIVER LEE NAVIGATION - Southern Volume -
Limehouse basin to Hackney Marsh. 5 walks on the Regent Canal, Hertford Union and Limehouse Cut. Including Three Mills and its rivers. The guide also details a 28 mile End to End walk along the Navigation. 68 pages. 10 maps, 30 photographs.
ISBn 1-903627-74-5 £7.95

EPPING FOREST CHALLENGE WALK - 21 MILES.
Starts and ends at Waltham Abbey and takes in the whole forest. 44 pages. 6 maps. 10 photos £7.95
ISBN 978-0-9553691-0-0

"St. ALBANS WAY" - 26 mile Pilgrims walk from Waltham Abbey to St. Alban's Cathedral.
£7.95
ISBN 978-0-9553691-3-1

NORTH LONDON - THE THREE BOROUGH CHALLENGE WALK - 21 MILES
A walk linking together the three boroughs of Enfield, Barnet and Haringey.
A magnificent countryside walk. Certificate for the successful.
A5. 40 pages. Full colour book.
ISBN 978-0-955651 1-9-9
£7.95

NEW - SHORT CIRCULAR WALKS IN EPPING DISTRICT

NEW LONDON WALK GUIDES

WALKING THE CANALS OF LONDON

Nine walks fully exploring - The Regents Canal, Grand Union Canal (Paddington Branch), River Thames and Isle of Dogs and the "London Canal Loop".
A5 wire bound. 108 pages. 13 maps. 95 b/w photographs.

£10.95 ISBN 978-0-9553691-2-4

WALKING THE STREETS OF LONDON

7 historical short walks - 2 to 6 miles long and allowing - 4 TO 5 HOURS - in the city with basic themes -

"The Great Fire', "Wigs & Pens".
The Good and Gracious".
"The Royal Palaces", "The Hot Spots",
"Bridges, Boats and Dungeons".
"Monks, murder, punishment and poetry".

A5 wire bound. 112 pages. 9 maps. 84 b/w photographs.

£10.95 ISBN 978-0-9553691-1-7

LONDON INTERFAITH WALKS - Vol. One

Seven walks in London to all the major religious sites.
Themed walks - Christian, Buddhist, Hindu etc.
. A5 Wire bound. 112 pages. 10 maps 130 photos.
£10.95
ISBN 978-0-9568044-3-3

See all our books on our website - www.johnmerrillwalkguides.com

THE AIM OF THE BOOK

The aim of this book was simply to walk every waymarked path within the confines of London and it's borough's and within the M25. There are a surprising number of routes, as this book demonstrates; combined there are some 600 miles of walking.

All the walks in this book can be done at your own pace; you don't have to walk the whole individual walk in a day. You can do in stages for there is always much to see and admire on the way. At the back of the book is a walk log so you can record when you walked each route.

The last walk in the book is my own creation - A walk for peace - and is a walk for quiet contemplation, while visiting three unique Buddhist sites.

ISBN978-0-9556511-3-7 £14.95 184 pages. 50 maps, 30 b/w photos.

Illustrated lectures
by
John N. Merrill

Lectures on
his major walks are available.
For further information
and bookings,
write to John Merrill at

THE JOHN MERRILL
FOUNDATION
32, Holmesdale,
Waltham Cross,
Hertfordshire
EN8 8QY
England

Tel/Fax 01992 - 762776
e-mail - marathonhiker@aol.com
www.johnmerrillwalkguides.com

Illustrated Lectures include -

" WALKING AROUND LONDON" - a brief look at walking in the city and countryside around London, some 1,800 miles of walking. - Capital Ring, Canals, London Loop,River Thames, New River, Pymmes Brook Trail & Jubilee Walkway, The Wandle Trail, the River Stort and Lee Navigations and Lee Valley Walk.

"WALKING MY WAY" - Why I walk and some of walks I have done - a hilarious but exhausting talk, from more than 182,000 miles of walking!

"WALKING THE CHESOPEAKE & OHIO CANAL - 250 miles from Washington D.C. to Cumberland, Maryland, USA.

"NORTH TO SANTIAGO via FATIMA" - 650 mile pilgrim's walk to Santiago de Compostelo, through Portugal.

"FOLLOW THE BLUE BLAZE" - Walking around the Buckeye Trail in Ohio, USA.1,300 miles - the first person to walk the complete trail in one continuous walk.

"Promoting walking, Pilgrimages, and understanding the countryside."

OTHER JOHN MERRILL WALK BOOKS

CIRCULAR WALK GUIDES -

SHORT CIRCULAR WALKS IN THE PEAK DISTRICT - VOL. 1,2, 3 AND 9
CIRCULAR WALKS IN WESTERN PEAKLAND
SHORT CIRCULAR WALKS IN THE STAFFORDSHIRE MOORLANDS
SHORT CIRCULAR WALKS - TOWNS & VILLAGES OF THE PEAK DISTRICT
SHORT CIRCULAR WALKS AROUND MATLOCK
SHORT CIRCULAR WALKS IN "PEAK PRACTICE COUNTRY."
SHORT CIRCULAR WALKS IN THE DUKERIES
SHORT CIRCULAR WALKS IN SOUTH YORKSHIRE
SHORT CIRCULAR WALKS IN SOUTH DERBYSHIRE
SHORT CIRCULAR WALKS AROUND BUXTON
SHORT CIRCULAR WALKS AROUND WIRKSWORTH
SHORT CIRCULAR WALKS IN THE HOPE VALLEY
40 SHORT CIRCULAR WALKS IN THE PEAK DISTRICT
CIRCULAR WALKS ON KINDER & BLEAKLOW
SHORT CIRCULAR WALKS IN SOUTH NOTTINGHAMSHIRE
SHORT CIRCULAR WALKS IN CHESHIRE
SHORT CIRCULAR WALKS IN WEST YORKSHIRE
WHITE PEAK DISTRICT AIRCRAFT WRECKS
CIRCULAR WALKS IN THE DERBYSHIRE DALES
SHORT CIRCULAR WALKS FROM BAKEWELL
SHORT CIRCULAR WALKS IN LATHKILL DALE
CIRCULAR WALKS IN THE WHITE PEAK
SHORT CIRCULAR WALKS IN EAST DEVON
SHORT CIRCULAR WALKS AROUND HARROGATE
SHORT CIRCULAR WALKS IN CHARNWOOD FOREST
SHORT CIRCULAR WALKS AROUND CHESTERFIELD
SHORT CIRCULAR WALKS IN THE YORKS DALES - VOL 1 - SOUTHERN AREA.
SHORT CIRCULAR WALKS IN THE AMBER VALLEY (DERBYSHIRE)
SHORT CIRCULAR WALKS IN THE LAKE DISTRICT
SHORT CIRCULAR WALKS IN THE NORTH YORKSHIRE MOORS
SHORT CIRCULAR WALKS IN EAST STAFFORDSHIRE
LONG CIRCULAR WALKS IN THE PEAK DISTRICT - VOL.1, 2 , 3, 4 AND 5.
DARK PEAK AIRCRAFT WRECK WALKS
LONG CIRCULAR WALKS IN THE STAFFORDSHIRE MOORLANDS
LONG CIRCULAR WALKS IN CHESHIRE
WALKING THE TISSINGTON TRAIL
WALKING THE HIGH PEAK TRAIL
WALKING THE MONSAL TRAIL & SETT VALLEY TRAILS
PEAK DISTRICT WALKING - TEN "TEN MILER'S" - VOL ONE AND TWO
CLIMB THE PEAKS OF THE PEAK DISTRICT
PEAK DISTRICT WALK A MONTH VOLS ONE,TWO, THREE, FOUR, FIVE & SIX
TRAIN TO WALK VOL. ONE - THE HOPE VALLEY LINE
DERBYSHIRE LOST VILLAGE WALKS -VOL ONE AND TWO.
CIRCULAR WALKS IN DOVEDALE AND THE MANIFOLD VALLEY
CIRCULAR WALKS AROUND GLOSSOP
WALKING THE LONGDENDALE TRAIL
WALKING THE UPPER DON TRAIL
SHORT CIRCULAR WALKS IN CANNOCK CHASE
CIRCULAR WALKS IN THE DERWENT VALLEY
WALKING THE TRAILS OF NORTH-EAST DERBYSHIRE
WALKING THE PENNINE BRIDLEWAY & CIRCULAR WALKS
SHORT CIRCULAR WALKS ON THE NEW RIVER & SOUTH-EAST HERTFORDSHIRE
SHORT CIRCULAR WALKS IN EPPING FOREST
WALKING THE STREETS OF LONDON
LONG CIRCULAR WALKS IN EASTERN HERTFORDSHIRE
LONG CIRCULAR WALKS IN WESTERN HERTFORDSHIRE
WALKS IN THE LONDON BOROUGH OF ENFIELD
WALKS IN THE LONDON BOROUGH OF BARNET
WALKS IN THE LONDON BOROUGH OF HARINGEY
WALK IN THE LONDON BOROUGH OF WALTHAM FOREST
SHORT CIRCULAR WALKS AROUND HERTFORD
THE BIG WALKS OF LONDON
SHORT CIRCULAR WALKS AROUND BISHOP'S STORTFORD
SHORT CIRCULAR WALKS AROUND EPPING DISTRICT
CIRCULAR WALKS IN THE BOROUGH OF BROXBOURNE
LONDON INTERFAITH WALKS - VOL 1 AND VOL. 2
LONG CIRCULAR WALKS IN THE NORTH CHILTERNS
SHORT CIRCULAR WALKS IN EASTERN HERTFORDSHIRE
WORCESTERSHIRE VILLAGE WALKS BY DES WRIGHT
WARWICKSHIRE VILLAGE WALKS BY DES WRIGHT
WALKING AROUND THE ROYAL PARKS OF LONDON

CANAL WALKS -

VOL 1 - DERBYSHIRE & NOTTINGHAMSHIRE
VOL 2 - CHESHIRE & STAFFORDSHIRE
VOL 3 - STAFFORDSHIRE
VOL 4 - THE CHESHIRE RING
VOL 5 - THE GRANTHAM CANAL
VOL 6 - SOUTH YORKSHIRE
VOL 7 - THE TRENT & MERSEY CANAL
VOL 8 - WALKING THE DERBY CANAL RING
VOL 9 - WALKING THE LLANGOLLEN CANAL
VOL 10 - CIRCULAR WALKS ON THE CHESTERFIELD CANAL
VOL 11 - CIRCULAR WALKS ON THE CROMFORD CANAL
VOL.13 - SHORT CIRCULAR WALKS ON THE RIVER LEE NAVIGATION -VOL. 1 - NORTH
VOL. 14 - SHORT CIRCULAR WALKS ON THE RIVER STORT NAVIGATION
VOL.15 - SHORT CIRCULAR WALKS ON THE RIVER LEE NAVIGATION - VOL. 2 - SOUTH
VOL. 16 - WALKING THE CANALS OF LONDON
VOL 17 - WALKING THE RIVER LEE NAVIGATION
VOL. 20 - SHORT CIRCULAR WALKS IN THE COLNE VALLEY
VOL 21 - THE BLACKWATER & CHELMER NAVIGATION - END TO END.
VOL. 22 - NOTTINGHAM'S LOST CANAL BY BERNARD CHELL.
VOL. 23 - WALKING THE RIVER WEY & GODALMING NAVIAGTIONS END TO END

JOHN MERRILL DAY CHALLENGE WALKS -

WHITE PEAK CHALLENGE WALK
THE HAPPY HIKER - WHITE PEAK - CHALLENGE WALK NO.2
DARK PEAK CHALLENGE WALK
PEAK DISTRICT END TO END WALKS
STAFFORDSHIRE MOORLANDS CHALLENGE WALK
THE LITTLE JOHN CHALLENGE WALK
YORKSHIRE DALES CHALLENGE WALK

NORTH YORKSHIRE MOORS CHALLENGE WALK
LAKELAND CHALLENGE WALK
THE RUTLAND WATER CHALLENGE WALK
MALVERN HILLS CHALLENGE WALK
THE SALTER'S WAY
THE SNOWDON CHALLENGE
CHARNWOOD FOREST CHALLENGE WALK
THREE COUNTIES CHALLENGE WALK (PEAK DISTRICT).
CAL-DER-WENT WALK BY GEOFFREY CARR,
THE QUANTOCK WAY
BELVOIR WITCHES CHALLENGE WALK
THE CARNEDDAU CHALLENGE WALK
THE SWEET PEA CHALLENGE WALK
THE LINCOLNSHIRE WOLDS - BLACK DEATH - CHALLENGE WALK
JENNIFER'S CHALLENGE WALK
THE EPPING FOREST CHALLENGE WALK
THE THREE BOROUGH CHALLENGE WALK - NORTH LONDON
THE HERTFORD CHALLENGE WALK

INSTRUCTION & RECORD -
HIKE TO BE FIT.....STROLLING WITH JOHN
THE JOHN MERRILL WALK RECORD BOOK
HIKE THE WORLD - JOHN MERRILL'S GUIDE TO WALKING & BACKPACKING.

MULTIPLE DAY WALKS -
THE RIVERS'S WAY
PEAK DISTRICT: HIGH LEVEL ROUTE
PEAK DISTRICT MARATHONS
THE LIMEY WAY
THE PEAKLAND WAY
COMPO'S WAY BY ALAN HILEY
THE BRIGHTON WAY

THE PILGRIM WALKS SERIES -
THE WALSINGHAM WAY - ELY TO WALSINGHAM - 72 MILES
THE WALSINGHAM WAY - KINGS LYNN TO WALSINGHAM - 35 MILES
TURN LEFT AT GRANJA DE LA MORERUELA - 700 MILES
NORTH TO SANTIAGO DE COMPOSTELA, VIA FATIMA - 650 MILES
ST. OLAV'S WAY - OSLO TO TRONDHEIM - 400 MILES
ST. WINEFRIDE'S WAY - ST. ASAPH TO HOLYWELL
ST. ALBANS WAY - WALTHAM ABBEY TO ST. ALBANS - 26 MILES
ST. KENELM TRAIL BY JOHN PRICE - CLENT HILLS TO WINCHCOMBE - 60 MILES
DERBYSHIRE PILGRIMAGES
LONDON TO CANTERBURY- 75 MILES
LONDON TO ST. ALBANS - 36 MILES
LONDON TO WALSINGHAM - 194 MILES
FOLKESTONE, HYTHE TO CANTERBURY - 25 MILES
THE JOHN SCHORNE PEREGRINATIONS - 27 MILES BY M. MOONEY
ST CEDD'S PILGRIMAGE WALK - 24 MILES
ST BIRINIUS PILGRIMAGE WALK - 26 MILES
OUR LADY OF ULTING PILGRIMAGE WALK - 16 MILES
OUR LADY OF CAVERSHAM PILGRIMAGE WALK - 38 MILES
THE MANDEVILLE MONKS WAY - 32 MILES
THE ESSEX PRIORIES WAY - 20 MILES
WALKING THE CAMMINO DI ASSISI - 320 KM.
A FUNERAL CELEBRANT'S DIARY
THE AYLESFORD PILGRIMAGE
THREE SOUTH-EAST OUR LADY PILGRIMAGE WALKS.

COAST WALKS & NATIONAL TRAILS -
ISLE OF WIGHT COAST PATH
PEMBROKESHIRE COAST PATH
THE CLEVELAND WAY
WALKING ANGELSEY'S COASTLINE.
WALKING THE COASTLINE OF THE CHANNEL ISLANDS
THE ISLE OF MAN COASTAL PATH - *"THE WAY OF THE GULL."*
A WALK AROUND HAYLING ISLAND
A WALK AROUND THE ISLE OF SHEPPEY
A WALK AROUND THE ISLE OF JERSEY
WALKING AROUND THE ISLANDS OF ESSEX

DERBYSHIRE & PEAK DISTRICT HISTORICAL GUIDES -
A TO Z GUIDE OF THE PEAK DISTRICT
DERBYSHIRE INNS - AN A TO Z GUIDE
HALLS AND CASTLES OF THE PEAK DISTRICT & DERBYSHIRE
TOURING THE PEAK DISTRICT & DERBYSHIRE BY CAR
DERBYSHIRE FOLKLORE
PUNISHMENT IN DERBYSHIRE
CUSTOMS OF THE PEAK DISTRICT & DERBYSHIRE
WINSTER - A SOUVENIR GUIDE
ARKWRIGHT OF CROMFORD
LEGENDS OF DERBYSHIRE
DERBYSHIRE FACTS & RECORDS
TALES FROM THE MINES BY GEOFFREY CARR
PEAK DISTRICT PLACE NAMES BY MARTIN SPRAY
DERBYSHIRE THROUGH THE AGES - VOL 1 -DERBYSHIRE IN PREHISTORIC TIMES
SIR JOSEPH PAXTON
FLORENCE NIGHTINGALE
JOHN SMEDLEY
BONNIE PRINCE CHARLIE & 20 MILE WALK.
THE STORY OF THE EARLS AND DUKES OF DEVONSHIRE

JOHN MERRILL'S MAJOR WALKS -
TURN RIGHT AT LAND'S END
WITH MUSTARD ON MY BACK
TURN RIGHT AT DEATH VALLEY
EMERALD COAST WALK
I CHOSE TO WALK - WHY I WALK ETC.
A WALK IN OHIO - 1,310 MILES AROUND THE BUCKEYE TRAIL.
I AM GUIDED - THE STORY OF JOHN'S LIFE.

SKETCH BOOKS -
SKETCHES OF THE PEAK DISTRICT

COLOUR BOOK:-
THE PEAK DISTRICT.......SOMETHING TO REMEMBER HER BY.

OVERSEAS GUIDES -
HIKING IN NEW MEXICO - VOL I - THE SANDIA AND MANZANO MOUNTAINS.
VOL 2 - HIKING "BILLY THE KID" COUNTRY. VOL 4 - N.W. AREA - " HIKING INDIAN COUNTRY."
"WALKING IN DRACULA COUNTRY" - ROMANIA.
WALKING THE TRAILS OF THE HONG KONG ISLANDS.

VISITOR GUIDES - MATLOCK . BAKEWELL. ASHBOURNE.

Why I walk

I am often asked why I walk and to be truthfull it is not easy to answer. I believe that walking gives you total freedom and at the same time getting some exercise without causing injuries like jogging. Freedom means the choice of walking at your own pace through a variety of countryside and looking and learning its secrets as you pass through. Freedom means the basics of life and you are master of your own destiny.

When I set off for the day I carry all I need on my back, be it for a day walk or an extended walk over days or months. I leave behind the trappings of modern life and break many of the accepted rules of walking, by walking alone, not informing anyone of where I am going and what my expected return is. I feel such niceties are restrictive and hinder one's freedom to dwell on places or extend the walk. I admit one must be careful and if conditions detrioate one must descend or seek shelter. Walking alone and facing the problems on the way enable one to know oneself totally and know how one reacts to situations and one's limitations. I don't carry a mobile phone for this is a trapping of modern life. To be out walking in solitude and suddenly the phone rings is an alarming thought; how can one be at peace with the countryside?

I walk not just for health but to see and explore an area of countryside. To follow a path by a stream and see a kingfisher flash by, or watch a dipper bobbing up and down on a rock are one of the delights and enchanting moments on a walk. To walk in Spring and see the different flowers emerging, the birds gathering twigs for their nests, the trees in bud and new leaves unfolding bring added pleasure to the scene. To walk into a village and look at the houses as you past, see the date stone or see a cheese press or stocks help to bring the village alive and see its past history. To look at the hall or other principal building, the inn with an unusual name makes one want to know more and perhaps at a later date a visit to the local history department of the nearby library to discover more. The church - the open book of village life - always deserves exploration. To wander around the gravestones and see the dates and inscriptions. To walk inside and see the ancient font or old tomb gives greater understanding to the walk.

I walk in the minimum of clothes for freedom. Only in winter do I wear long trousers preferring to wear shorts and a T shirt most of the time. Even in rain I prefer walking in shorts with a poncho keeping dry but allowing maximum movement and freedom. Boots are worn whatever the walk but a lightweight pair for use in a dry summer and a more heavier and leather boot for winter or rain. A camera and binoculars to record and see distant mountains or birds; and for seeking out the blazed route ahead or for locating a stile.

Whilst there is the undeniable joy of exploring the area being walked through there is the added challenge of effort and fitness. I don't believe I walk fast just a steady 3 miles (5km) per hour, which I maintain without a rest during the day. I walk anything between 8 to 12 hours everyday, for days on end. I enjoy the mastery of walking up hill and dale and being able to push myself to walk further. Alternatively knowing I have thirty miles to walk, that day, and being able to pace oneself and complete the task still feeling fit and no pain. Knowing also that I can walk further if necessary. I don't train for a long walk simply preferring to set off and walk myself in as I progress.

Walking is spiritual. Yes, I believe in God and I have prayed often on a walk for help and guidance and have never been let down. I have also thanked him for the wonders I have seen on the way. Who cannot be moved when ascending to a pass and seeing sprawled out before you some incredibly beautiful scene. Who can wonder that after ten days alone in the wilderness that I reach the precise point I have been walking to. Yes, it is skill but I have been helped along the way and "shown" the route.

Walking is addictive but not compulsive. I find no hardship in walking day after day a marathon or more with forty pounds or more on my back. I never want to give up and can't wait to start again in the morning. The return from a long walk means a day walk has little meaning and for a while I peer out of the window but find it hard to put on the boots. But after a while as I have readjusted back a little I become restless and "angry" and put the boots on and walk for a few hours. If after that I have not been out for a few days I start to get withdrawal symptoms and have to break free and go for a walk.

So walking for me is a way of life, giving me the freedom to explore the countryside at my own pace. No other hobby or job gives you so much - exercise, experience, delight, discovery, adventure and exploration at such a minimal cost. It is man's simplest form of travel - on foot - and the only way to explore the world.

My footprint.

LOST NAVIGATION ARM

Just to the north of Enfield Lock is the Naviagtion arm leading to the Small Arms Factory, where the famous Lee & Enfield rifles were made. Today Enfield Island Village - a large housing estate - covers the factory area of the Small Arms factory. Today reached via a road bridge close to The Greyhound Inn at Grid Ref: 373987.

The arm into the factory was at Grid Ref: 374993. The location is approximately 1/4 mile north from the Island bridge. Here on a lefthand bend in the navigation are the remains of a bridge and pipes on either side of the navigation. By ascending to the top of the bridge on the left, you have a good view of the arm, which cannot be seen from the towpath.

The basin in Island Village with part of the former Small Arms factory buildings behind; now used as a fitness centre.

The remains of the Navigation Arm in Enfield Island Village.

Former Water Tower in the Small Arms Factory; Enfield Island Village.

THE JOHN MERRILL FOUNDATION LONG DISTANCE WALKING CHARTER FOR THE U.K.

1. All path signs to be made of wood and clearly state the right of way designation and destination with correct mileage/kilometres. Individuality of design, logo or symbols is to be encouraged. Variety is the spice of life!

2. Wooden stiles are preferred to kissing gates. Kissing gates have a fatal flaw – many are not wide enough to allow a backpacker with his pack to get in and out of. For half the year the central area is wet and muddy. The metal bar stiles with a wide base that narrow at the top should be abolished; they are not suitable for backpacker use – all have to take the rucksacks off to get through.
   S.O.S. - Save our stiles.

3. All long distance routes to clearly state the start and end of the route on the ground, with an overall map showing the route at each end. Registration boxes at either end for signing in and out.

4. All temporary path closures should be notified from the nearest road and not at the start of the particular path, resulting in having to walk back. The diversion or temporary alternative route should be clearly well signed.

5. Every walker should be trained to read a map, use a compass, and calculate a grid reference. The dependence of modern technology is to be encouraged – but learn the basic skills.

6. All long distance walkers should wear well broken in and good fitting boots with two pairs of socks; and carry the minimum basics in a suitable framed rucksack.

7. Take your rubbish home.

8. Take only pictures.

9. Admire the flowers but do not pick them.

10. Say "hello" to all walkers that you pass.

11. Leave your music centre at home so you can enjoy the sounds of the countryside.

12. All footpaths should be regularly cleared of brambles, nettles, blow downs, and overhanging branches to allow the walker to pass through comfortably. Paths should be natural earth, not gravel, tarmac or slab.

July 2015.

WHY I WALK *by Revd. John N. Merrill*

I walk for the exercise; to stretch my legs and muscles; to suck in the fresh air and be free in the wide, wide world, as I walk upon Mother Earth.

I walk to see the trees; that sway in the breeze. To watch the leaves flutter in summer and to walk through on the ground in November. I observe the quietness of winter and watch the buds form ready to emerge when it is their time.

I walk to see the wild flowers; the wood anemones, the blue bells, red campion, and orchids that grow in Spring and early summer.

I walk to listen to the birds that sing in the hedgerows and trees. The friendly Robin is not far away, the started Jay or motionless heron standing at the waters edge. A sudden flash of blue as a kingfisher shoots by.

I walk to see the wild animals; the red fox, the deer, the squirrel and the insects and butterflies, like the dragonfly and red admiral butterfly.

I walk to see the views; to ascend a lofty peak and sit upon the summit surveying everything below, like an eagle high in the air.

I walk for solitude; peace and quiet, to go back to the basics of life, where it is just man and the elements.

I walk in the sunshine, the rain, snow and wind. All has its own beauty and characteristic. All are the cycles of life. I admire the cloudless sky and the rolling clouds of wind and storm.

I walk to see the work of man and God, knowing that we are all connected. Everything has its own beauty.

As the sun sets and I walk home, I know I have lived and experienced a full day, witnessing the whole spectrum of life. I am grateful, very grateful, that God gave me two fine legs, a healthy heart and good lungs to see paradise on Earth.

May the sun bring you new energy by day,
May the moon softly restore you by night,
May the rain wash away your worries,
May the breeze blow new strength into your being,
May you walk gently through the world and
Know it's beauty all the days of your life.

Apache blessing.

Look at the tees,
Look at the birds,
Look at the clouds,
Look at the stars ....
And if you have eyes
you will be able to see
that the whole of
existence is joyful.

Osho

THE JOHN MERRILL MINISTRY

- a universal monk - embracing & honouring all faiths & none.

John has been following his own spiritual path all his life, and is guided. He was brought up as a Christian and confirmed at the age of 13. He then went to a Quaker Boarding School for five years and developed his love for the countryside and walking. He became fascinated with Tibet and whilst retaining his Christian roots, became immersed in Buddhism. For four years he studied at the Tara Buddhist Centre in Derbyshire. He progressed into Daoism and currently attends the Chinese Buddhist Temple (Pure Land Tradition) in London. With his thirst for knowledge and discovery he paid attention to other faiths and appreciated their values. Late in life he decided it was time to reveal his spiritual beliefs and practices and discovered the Interfaith Seminary.

'When the pupil is ready, the teacher will appear'. (Buddhist saying).

Here for two years he learnt in more depth the whole spectrum of faiths , including Jainism, Paganism, Mother Earth, Buddhism, Hinduism, Islam, Judaism, Sikhism, Celtic Worship and Shamanism. This is an ongoing exploration without end. He embraces all faiths, for all have a beauty of their own. All paths/faiths lead to one goal/truth. On July 17th. 2010 he was Ordained as a Multi-faith Minister.

'May you go in peace, with joy in your heart
and may the divine be always at your side.'

Using his knowledge and experience he combines many faiths into a simple, caring and devoted services, individually made for each specific occasion, with dignity and honour.
He conducts special Ceremonies -

Popular Funeral Celebrant and member of the Natural Death Society.

* Funerals * Memorial Services * Sermons * Weddings *Civil Partnerships * Baby Blessings & Naming
* Rites of Passage * Healing Ceremonies * Pilgimages * Inspirational Talks
Qigong Teacher. Reiki Prationer.

For further information Contact John on -
Tel/Fax: 01992 - 762776 Mobile. 07910 889429
Email - buddhaonfoot@mail.com
Ministry site -www.thejohnmerrillministry.co.uk
All Faiths church - www.londoninterfaithchurch.co.uk

Revd. John N. Merrill, HonMUni